Same Side SELLING

A RADICAL APPROACH TO BREAK THROUGH SALES BARRIERS

Ian Altman
#1 Amazon Bestselling Author of
Upside Down Selling

Jack Quarles
#1 Amazon Bestselling Author of
How Smart Companies Save Money

IDEAPRESS
PUBLISHING

Published in the United States by Ideapress Publishing.

IDEAPRESS PUBLISHING
www.ideapresspublishing.com

All trademarks are the property of their respective companies.

Cover Design & Page Layout by PanoGraphics

Cataloging-in-Publication Data is on file with the
Library of Congress.

Second Printing
ISBN: 978-1-940858-06-7
Library of Congress Control Number: 2014934405

PRINTED IN THE UNITED STATES OF AMERICA BY
Selby Marketing

SPECIAL SALES
Ideapress Books are available at a special discount for bulk purchases for
sales promotions and premiums, or for use in corporate training programs.
Special editions, including personalized covers, custom forewards, corporate
imprints and custom bonus content are also available. For more details, email
info@ideapresspublishing.com or info@SameSideSelling.com

*No animals were harmed in the writing, printing or distribution
of this book. The trees, unfortunately, were not so lucky.*

For more ideas on how to be successful with
Same Side Selling, visit:

www.SameSideSelling.com

Acknowledgments

Catherine Oliver's editing was brilliant. We credit her with great improvements in the clarity, organization, and readability of our work. Tim Ingle was a keen set of eyes and our technical wizard. Denise Solan kept us focused and made sure that the world would get to hear about our work.

It was through Derek and Melanie Coburn, the creators of the group Cadre, that we met. Cadre provided the fertile ground for friendship and collaboration that inspired us to work together.

We want to give special thanks and acknowledgment to our respective spouses, Deborah and Linda, as well as our children. They give us constant support and inspiration, and they put up with the phone calls, meetings, and interruptions that led us to Same Side Selling.

Table of Contents

Introduction

A Better Way to Sell (and Buy)

Every day, buyers and sellers speak with each other. Many of those conversations lead to sales and high satisfaction. But far too often, the buyer-seller discussion leads to such challenges as mutual mistrust, poor communication, misunderstanding, confusion, and disappointment.

Obviously these challenges are bad for the seller and the buyer, yet they seem to be more the norm than the exception. Why?

In most cases, the symptoms of these challenges reveal a deeper problem that we call the adversarial trap. In the adversarial trap, the buyer-seller dynamic can develop into an us-versus-them mentality, implying that one "side" can win only if the other loses. The *adversarial trap* leads to long decision cycles, deception, and the withholding of information for the buyer and the seller. A drawn-out, contentious dynamic is in neither party's best interest.

There is a better way to sell. Great selling should not be adversarial. (Neither should great buying.)

How This Book Started

Ian and Jack met at a networking event. Ian is well known for helping companies achieve more success with selling, and Jack has a strong background in helping companies save money when they buy. Given their job titles, you might think they would be natural enemies, like the sheepdog and the wolf. Vivid stereotypes come to mind:

The sales pro—slick, manipulative, pushing buttons to cajole people into buying what they really don't need for exorbitant prices.

The procurement guy—controlling, power-hungry, solely focused on price and viewing everything as a commodity.

The traditional caricatures may be rooted in truth. But as Ian and Jack talked, they discovered that neither of them fit the stereotypical mold.

Ian spoke about *solving problems* more than about selling, and he discussed an integrity-based approach in which the goal is to get to the truth with prospects as soon as possible. Jack talked about the buyer benefit far more than the price, and about finding expert vendors that delivered the greatest value. Far from disagreeing and debating, Ian and Jack seemed to be using the same language and describing the same goal: making the selling process as efficient and productive as possible.

At some point, Ian remarked to Jack, "I wish all of my clients were selling to buyers who saw things the way you did."

Jack replied, "No kidding—I wish my clients could buy from salespeople who were practicing your approach."

Something clicked. It was a chocolate-in-the-peanut-butter moment. Could these two great tastes taste great together?

The historic relationship between buyers and sellers has progressed as a corporate arms race. The vendor employs a sales force; the buyer creates a purchasing group. The vendor hires a sales consultant; the buyer gets a procurement consultant. Tactic A drives Defense 1; Selling Trick B triggers Buying Trick 2. Eventually, each side takes on too many casualties. This antiquated style of selling might make you think of the old Stephen Wright joke: "I bought a humidifier and a de-humidifier. I put them in the same room and let them fight it out."

Getting on the Same Side

Picture a salesperson sitting down with a prospect in a meeting room. Where is the salesperson seated? Where is the prospect? If we asked you to draw a diagram of this meeting, it would almost certainly have the buyer and seller on opposite sides of the table. (OK, maybe not, if you've carefully noted the title of the book and the subhead above!)

This book is devoted to changing that picture so that the buyer and the seller are on the same side of the table. *Same Side Selling* will be helpful to you if any of these thoughts sound familiar:

- "I've got great things to sell to my clients, but my message seems to fall on deaf ears."
- "I'm tired of wrestling with my prospects."
- "I hate feeling mistrusted."
- "I can't figure out why my clients are reluctant to share information that would allow me to help them better."
- "My prospects are trying to convince me that everything we need to know is in the RFP, but we both know that's not true."
- "Why is it that every discussion seems to be focused on price, not value?"

The adversarial trap makes selling harder and more time-consuming, and it gives salespeople a bad reputation. We will address these frustrations throughout *Same Side Selling*, and we'll present an alternative approach that may fit better with your personality and ethics.

But the goal is not simply to feel good. The goal of *Same Side Selling* is to solve important challenges for clients, resulting in business for you and positive outcomes for them. (And if you want to call that "selling," we're OK with that.)

A Different Type of Book on Selling

What makes *Same Side Selling* different from any other book we could find on this topic is that it is co-authored by people on both "sides": a salesman (Ian) and a procurement and expense management veteran who intimately understands how companies buy (Jack). The buyer's perspective is baked into every sentence of Same Side Selling, along with the seller's point of view.

What may come as a surprise — but probably shouldn't — is that Jack's buyer perspective and Ian's seller perspective rarely conflict, and what will feel better as a seller will also be more effective with buyers.

Terminology

Note that we will use the terms *buyer, customer, client*, and *prospect* to mean essentially the same thing: someone with whom you are doing business or hope to do business. Likewise, we will use the terms *challenge, problem*, and *issue* to refer to the matter with which you can help the buyer. We don't want terminology to distract from the main focus of using your offerings and expertise to help people and companies move ahead with their goals.

How the Book Is Organized

Same Side Selling presents a tactical approach to escape the adversarial trap at each step of the sales process and throughout the client engagement. These steps might all be covered in a single thirty-minute conversation, or they might unfold over months, depending on the context of the sale. Following is an overview of what you will discover in each chapter of *Same Side Selling*.

Chapter 1: Stop Playing Games

Whether you like it or not, buyers and sellers get caught in adversarial games that pit one against the other. Even the terminology and tactics take their lead from war and battle metaphors. In contrast, the Same Side Selling mindset puts the buyer and seller on the same side of the table. Instead of contemplating a battle, think of selling and buying as two people working together assembling a puzzle.

Chapter 2: Be Unique

For a salesperson, trying to be all things to all buyers is a losing approach. The foundation of collaborative selling is differentiation. You can be unique in the value you offer, even when you are selling something that many others sell.

Chapter 3: Narrow Your Market

Too many sellers spend far too much energy pursuing weak opportunities. Effective qualification begins with understanding why a prospect would buy. Discover tools and questions that will help you get to the why quickly.

Chapter 4: Get to the Truth

A seemingly hot prospect can become a lengthy, costly pursuit when the seller fails to uncover the truth about the buyer's urgency and readiness. To shorten the sales cycle, get to the truth efficiently and in a way that makes the buyer more likely to take action.

Chapter 5: Be an Educator

Amid oceans of information, sellers often fail to effectively educate buyers. Discover how to educate buyers, learn tactics for sharing information successfully, and learn the difference between providing information and giving free consulting.

Chapter 6: Focus on the Fit

When you're educating buyers, details can sometimes overtake the message and distract from the overall value of the process. Follow a few simple principles to keep the discussion in the right place.

Chapter 7: Don't Force the Fit

Too many sellers push a deal forward even when it is not a great fit, causing short-term pain and slowing long-term growth. Restraint is the best long-term strategy and can even be a useful selling tool.

Chapter 8: Sell Value, Not Price

Despite good relationships and processes, sellers often find themselves combating a "low bid wins" mentality. You can free buyers from a fixation on the purchase price by helping them see value and total costs.

Chapter 9: Deliver Impact

In the sales role, it can be easy to forget that a contract is not the finish line. The deal is not done until the client has realized the outcome he thought he was buying.

* * *

Whether you are selling products, services, or some combination of both, following the guidance in this book should ensure that you and your client or prospect are working together on the same side of the table.

That is the whirlwind tour. Every chapter ends with suggestions for taking action, and we have provided chapter summaries at the end of the book. But please don't miss all the words in the middle. That's where you'll find stories, examples, scripts, and explanations that we believe will help you achieve extraordinary success with your clients and prospects.

If you agree that effective sales should be about collaboration, not about winning a battle, then let's go!

—Ian and Jack

CHAPTER 1
Stop Playing Games

Bighorn sheep will often charge each other at full force until one of them either runs away or loses consciousness. Dueling antelope rush head to head with sharp, pointed horns to demonstrate their superiority over others in the herd.

Too often, buyers and sellers engage in a similar adversarial dance. Each party positions their business to defeat their perceived opponent. While this approach might make sense with respect to competition, it can also prevail when businesses relate to customers. Though neither buyer nor seller is likely to lose consciousness, a combative posture causes headaches, produces inefficiencies, and rarely results in a positive outcome for either party. Whether you are a buyer beating up the seller, or a seller trying to get the buyer to purchase something his organization doesn't need, you are positioned for failure.

Even if you are not guilty of these evil practices, the dastardly people who came before you have already poisoned the well. As someone with a sales or business development role in your organization, you may have experienced the following:

- A new acquaintance rolls his eyes or makes an awkward joke when he learns that you have a role in sales.
- A prospective client is suspicious of the questions you ask and refuses to answer.
- You get caught up in the blame game when something minor goes wrong with a client.

From a buying perspective, many of us have endured at least one of these situations:

- The sales guy sells one thing to the customer and then tries to deliver something different from what was purchased.

- A vendor presents alleged expertise on a project, but you later learn that the company has no relevant experience.
- A company increases prices after it's too late for you to switch vendors.
- A vendor's results fall short, and the vendor says it's your fault.

These experiences and others like them are all symptoms of a problem that we call "the adversarial trap." The adversarial trap causes buyers and sellers to work against each other instead of collaborating. If you have spent any time selling, you have probably found yourself in this form of business purgatory. Not only was it uncomfortable, but it probably also resulted in a less-than-ideal outcome.

Fortunately, there is a way out of the adversarial trap. It starts with changing the traditional mindset of both sellers and buyers. Then you can stop playing games.

The Old Metaphor: Selling Is a Game

Traditionally, the sales profession has attracted a competitive personality. To some extent, that is to be expected given the nature of the job.

Selling is more readily measurable than other business disciplines, such as management or customer service. In many circles, the sales function is viewed as "a numbers game" for which both inputs and outputs are easily tracked quantitatively: prospects, cold calls, meetings, demos, customers, projects, revenue, and so on.

It's no surprise that a field that is so numbers-focused attracts people who are numbers-oriented. What other parts of our society are dominated by numbers? An obvious connection is to the world of sports. In fact, the most common metaphor for selling and negotiating has been that of the game. How many of the top sales books of the last half-century feature the words *close*, *game*, or *win* in the title? How many coaches and athletes have written books about business success?

While the game metaphor has been passed along to generations of selling professionals, the metaphor has also transferred to the buyers. Many buyers now view the buying process as a game. The game mindset influences thinking and behavior before, during, and after the sale.

In a game, one side wins and the other side loses. An adversarial mindset is implicit from the start.

Making matters worse, many sellers, when faced with pressure to "hit their numbers," seem more interested in selling what they have in their bags than in finding the best solutions for their prospects. Once buyers have been burned once or twice with solutions that did not fit their needs, they stop trusting the sales professionals. It should come as no surprise that some buyers have determined that the best way to protect themselves is to keep the salespeople at arms' length and in the dark.

That reaction from buyers brings us full circle. The selling-as-a-game idea has reinforced itself as it has traveled from thought leaders to salespeople to buyers and back to salespeople. The adversarial trap now appears virtually anywhere that products are bought and sold, and the dominant metaphor continues to be the game.

Our aim is to replace the adversarial trap with a cooperative, collaborative mindset. We also want to replace the old metaphor of selling as a game.

The New Metaphor: Selling Is a Puzzle

We would like to bury the metaphor of competing in a game and replace it with the metaphor of solving a puzzle. Let's compare the two:

> *Selling is not a game.*
>
> In a game, you are playing.
>
> In a game, there is a winner and a loser. Over time, you build a win-loss record.
>
> In a game, you sit across from your opponent, trying to win.

> *Selling is a puzzle.*
>
> With a puzzle, you are solving.
>
> With a puzzle, you create something. Over time, you build a history of value.
>
> With a puzzle, you sit on the same side, determining if pieces are a good fit.

The puzzle metaphor is simple, but adopting it in practice is not easy. A puzzle-based, *Same Side Selling* approach has implications for every step of the sales process and the client relationship, as we detail in the following chapters.

The first step of Same Side Selling is to embrace the idea of solving a puzzle instead of playing a game.

A Deeply Entrenched Mindset

You may be tempted to think "OK, they want us to collaborate; I get it" and flip to the next chapter. But before you do, it's worth exploring just how prevalent game-based thinking is, perhaps even at your company.

Competing Against Other Companies

As you look at your own industry, it is probably standard practice to define your company in a competitive manner. Have you heard any of these phrases recently?

- "We're third in market share …"
- "This is our win ratio for RFP responses …"
- "Our main competition is …"
- "We need more shots on goal …" or "more at-bats …"

The thinking behind this language is fully reasonable. There are specific situations in which only one company can "win" the business. We will explore this concept—and how to rise above it—in Chapter 2, Be Unique, and Chapter 3, Narrow Your Market. In the meantime, let's keep exploring how prevalent competitive game-based thinking is in your business.

Competing Against Customers

An overly competitive outlook often bleeds into relationships with prospects or customers. This outlook shows up in the language often heard in reference to a company's clients:

- "We're competing against their internal capability."
- "They're cutting into our margin."
- "If they were more informed, they wouldn't need us."

- "If they don't adopt what we provide, that's their problem."

These statements reflect an attitude of us-versus-them, which implies a winner and a loser. That adversarial approach makes the selling process harder and less fruitful. In contrast, a puzzle-solving approach turns prospects into teammates.

Imagine that you and someone else are jointly assembling a puzzle. Each of you has a set of pieces. Now imagine how challenging it becomes if there is a barrier between the two of you. The other person can see the puzzle, but you have to rely on the descriptions of the pieces she needs to complete the puzzle. In that scenario, it could be that the puzzle pieces are not even for the same puzzle. You might work together for days or weeks before realizing that your pieces do not fit the other person's puzzle.

In Chapter 4, Get to the Truth, and Chapter 5, Be an Educator, we apply the puzzle-solving approach directly to sales conversations and explain how to exchange information in a way that keeps the buyer and seller on the same side.

Of course, the game mentality doesn't always originate from the seller. Current practices in corporate purchasing and procurement often fuel the adversarial fire. Through Requests for Proposals, Requests for Quotes, reverse auctions, and other sourcing techniques, buyers and their agents aim to drive all manner of purchases to commoditized, apples-to-apples comparisons. These competitive structures seem to favor the lowest cost and offer little opportunity for authentic conversation and differentiation. We explore that specific trap — and its remedies — in Chapter 8, Sell Value, Not Price.

A New Acronym, A New Focus

The idea of selling as a game is exquisitely illustrated in a well-known scene from the movie *Glengarry Glen Ross*. Alec Baldwin's character, Blake, breaks from a torrent of threats and braggadocio to refresh his sales team on the classic mnemonic *ABC: Always Be Closing*. The film, released in 1984, brought this high-pressure sales concept from the 1950s to the attention of the general public. Let's consider what it means.

To Always Be Closing means that you constantly keep a laser-like focus on finalizing the sale. Nothing else matters:

- What happens when you first meet a potential prospect? *Always Be Closing.*
- If she has objections or questions? *Always Be Closing.*
- When he brings a new stakeholder into the process? Always Be Closing.
- If the company might not be your optimal client? *Always Be Closing.*

ABC is all about making the sale.

Same Side Selling is first and foremost about finding the fit. Rather than looking to win as an individual or a company, the goal is to work with the prospect to create a picture that makes sense and looks right to everyone involved. For the new puzzle metaphor, we also need a new acronym.

FIT: Finding Impact Together

Same Side Selling can be summarized with the acronym FIT, which stands for *Finding Impact Together*. Finding Impact Together is a mantra that can be useful at nearly every stage of the sales process and customer relationship. FIT will be our conscience check and guiding star throughout the book, so let's unpack what it conveys, one word at a time. The implications of FIT are quite different from those of ABC.

Finding versus Closing

Finding means discovering. It often involves teaching, sharing, investigating, or diagnosing. It also means that the outcome is unknown: what you are seeking might be there or it might not.

Closing means getting to a signature and a customer. We are not arguing that closing is unimportant. But closing often implies cajoling, persuading, manipulating, and making something happen. Closing implies that you might create something even if it isn't there.

Impact

When you are solving a puzzle, finding the right pieces often takes considerable effort, but when they fit together, the result is clear and rewarding. The same is true when a well-defined need meets a well-crafted solution in the marketplace.

Impact is *not* about your product or service. What you are selling matters, but what's far more important is how your offering solves someone else's problem. It's not about you or your stuff. It's about the customer's problem and solving it. Impact applies to the issue worth solving, as well as to the solution you have envisioned. Finding impact means mutually agreeing on why the client needs help and what the likely results of your solution will be.

Together

Same Side Selling is collaborative and cooperative. Those are nice, friendly words, and they align with an integrity-based approach to sales. As we will discover, putting the client's perspective first yields better results with less effort.

Solving, Not Selling

Ian speaks frequently at business networking meetings. He often asks the question, "How many of you came here tonight hoping to meet someone who might lead to a sale?" When pressed to be honest, usually more than half of the people in the room raise their hands.

Then Ian follows up with question number two: "How many people came here today hoping that someone would try to sell you something?" Amid the laughter in the room, one or two jokers raise their hands (and are often then bombarded with business cards).

As the crowd does the math and realizes the mismatch between people eager to sell and those eager to buy, Ian asks a third question: "Seriously, now; how many of you would be happy to meet someone tonight who could help you solve one of your biggest business challenges? Raise your hand, and keep your hand up if you would be happy to pay for that help." Once again, the room is full of raised hands.

Take a minute and re-read the last three paragraphs. Consider again the difference between the second question and the third question. While no one wants to be sold something, nearly everyone could use help to solve a problem.

19

Being Helpful

The difference between selling and helping has huge implications for everyone in sales. The reality is that most prospects will quickly classify us into one of two categories: 1) we are trying to sell them something, or 2) we are there to determine if we can help them solve a problem.

Chris Brogan visits this theme often in his blog, which is consistently ranked among the most popular and influential business blogs. Brogan has summed up his philosophy of marketing success with these two words: "Be helpful." The advice seems simple but is worth repeating and adopting as a foundation of *Same Side Selling*.

To be helpful, you have to know where people need help. That means seeing the buyer's problems from the buyer's perspective.

> **Buyer's Perspective:** *Throughout the book we will present insights and quotes drawn from Jack's experience working with senior-level company decision makers. Of course, all of us are buyers, so as you read this book, we encourage you to consider how you would respond to a Same Side Selling approach as a buyer.*

It's About Their Problem, Not Your Solution

To be seen as a solver instead of a seller, you must deliberately demote "making the sale" to a secondary priority. The primary focus is on helping to solve the buyer's problem. This means that your product's features and your company's qualifications are relevant only so far as they solve the buyer's problems. (For more on that, see Chapter 6, Focus on the Fit.)

Elevating helpfulness above selling does not mean that you never sell or that you should run away at the first sign of an objection. However, if you have thoroughly investigated the buyer's challenge and determined that you do not have the right solution, it is far better to be candid than to keep pushing.

The following anecdote illustrates the difference between the ABC and FIT approaches:

> When Ian was the CEO of a software and consulting company, he accompanied Steve, one of his salespeople, on a meeting. They were meeting with a senior executive, Mary, at a large telecommunications company. Steve was trying to convince Mary that her company should purchase a $150,000 solution. Each time Mary asked if the solution could do something specific, Steve would start tap-dancing around the question and suggest that the solution could do anything the company needed. After hearing a few questions, Ian realized that the software was not right for the client.

> In a moment that shocked Steve, Ian said, "Mary, I don't think that our software is the right platform for what you are trying to do. I fear you'll have a one-off solution that will not scale enough. Can we discuss your needs a bit more so we can make a recommendation that is appropriate?" After an extensive discussion (Ian seems to remember Steve needing oxygen at this point), Mary said, "Based on everything we've discussed, have you built something like this before?" As much as Steve hoped that the answer would be "Yes," Ian said, "Not exactly. We've built similar solutions for insurance companies, manufacturers, and pharmaceu-

tical companies, but not this exact telecomm solution." Mary said, "Three vendors have told me they have something. But I've been doing this long enough to know that if it existed, I would have seen it. You are clearly looking out for us. What will it take for your team to build it?"

Ian told Mary, "It would cost about $750,000 just to build a pilot. Based on how you described your user community, I would not be surprised if the eventual solution cost between $2 million and $3 million. Just so you know, maintaining a system like this, with the number of users you described, costs our other clients more than $1 million per year." Mary thought for a moment and said, "How soon could you start?" The client ended up doing over $15 million of business with Ian's company over the next decade.

Several elements of this story relate to different chapters in this book. The bottom line, however, is that Mary and Ian were working on the same side of the table to find a solution to a problem that was costing Mary's company about $5 million annually.

Steve was thinking ABC, and Ian was thinking FIT. Thankfully, FIT prevailed.

The Game-Based Mentality Has to Change

The adversarial selling mentality is not just inefficient; it's quickly becoming ineffective. As the information age continues to advance and the function of buying becomes more mature, a game-based approach to selling will leave the seller with lower margins and the buyer with fewer options. We learned more about this from David Clevenger, VP of Corporate United, which helps hundreds of large companies manage suppliers and expenses:

> The strategic sourcing revolution appears to be at an end, with large corporate procurement departments finding it impossible to drive savings the same old way, and suppliers having no room left to move. The way of the future is collaborative sourcing, where the buyer and seller come together, share information, innovate, and find ways to economize. The companies that take this path will identify, quantify, and implement meaningful solutions, and those that don't will struggle to compete.

On the buyer's side or the seller's side, the future will be brightest for those who are Finding Impact Together. Are you ready to move to the Same Side?

Put Same Side Selling to Work

Both the buyer and the seller have traditionally viewed selling as a game. This us-versus-them mindset results in a far less efficient sales process. A better metaphor for selling is a puzzle. Instead of Always Be Closing, a better reminder is FIT—Finding Impact Together. By being helpful first and focusing on the buyer's challenge, a seller can stay on the same side as the buyer and avoid the adversarial trap.

✔ How did you learn about selling? Did your most important influences or trainers define selling more like a game or like a puzzle?

✔ Identify two of your clients with whom you have an adversarial relationship. On a scale of 0–10 (where 0 is stressful and 10 is comforting), how would you rate the experience of working with each of them? How would they rate the experience of working with you? Did the outcome of their purchase achieve its potential or fall short?

✔ Identify the last major sales opportunity that you lost. Did your team approach it as a game or as a puzzle? How might your actions have been different if you had treated that opportunity more as a puzzle?

✔ Identify two specific activities of your sales team that reinforce the game approach. Could either of those be changed to reflect a puzzle approach?

✔ Can you think of a situation when you worked with your client to find impact together, instead of just trying to sell something? What was the nature of the dialogue? Was it adversarial or cooperative? Was it more focused on price or less focused on price?

✔ Make a list of problems that your solution is exceptionally good at solving.

CHAPTER 2
Be Unique

In the first chapter we introduced the puzzle metaphor, the idea of solving a problem instead of pushing a sale, and the acronym FIT—Finding Impact Together. Of course, the word "fit" has a literal meaning that is just as relevant to Same Side Selling: the buyer's pieces and the seller's pieces must fit together. To arrive at this fit, sellers must know what pieces they hold and what makes them distinctive.

In this chapter, we discuss why it is crucial to differentiate your offerings. We'll also discuss how to define and present your uniqueness in the marketplace—even when you sell something that doesn't seem much different from what your competitors offer.

Standing Out from the Crowd Is Essential

The most successful sellers know exactly what they bring to the marketplace. They zero in on the areas where they can have the greatest impact for clients. Their offering is not shifting or vague; it is as clearly defined as the outline of a puzzle piece.

The Unique Positioning of the Cadre Networking Group

There is no shortage of networking groups in the Washington, D.C., metropolitan area. It's a region that appreciates the importance of being connected, and there are hundreds of organizations devoted to developing relationships that can be professionally helpful. In that context, the odds would seem to be against Derek and Melanie Coburn, who started a new group in 2011. Yet in less than two years, their group—called "cadre"—grew to capacity and became one of the most successful groups of its kind in the United States.

How did cadre stand out from the others? Derek and Melanie had a vision of how their group would be unique, and they clearly presented the vision to prospective candidates. To start with, cadre was labeled an "un-networking group." Then the founders explained why it was different: new members should not expect to close sales with other members of the group in the near term.

This approach is counterintuitive because for most people, the explicit purpose of a networking group is to generate sales. But Derek and Melanie weren't looking for *most people*. They were looking for established business owners and principals who were seeking high-quality relationships and professional or personal development and who were looking to give to others first.

The unique positioning led to extremely efficient marketing. In a mature, competitive field, cadre stood out as different and attractive to its target prospects.

Puzzle Pieces Are Distinctive

Same Side Selling requires a clear definition of your unique value proposition. You must understand which problems you can solve and which you cannot, who your best prospects are, and who would be better served by someone else.

The puzzle piece is a helpful reminder. Because of its distinctive shape, a puzzle piece is of great use where it fits—but only where it fits. In contrast, a building block can be defined by simple dimensions and be useful almost anywhere. Clay can be molded to fit in many places. But the puzzle piece has contours and limitations. When it is in the right place, the puzzle piece is essential. Otherwise, it is useless.

What You Sell Is Essential; What You Sell Is Useless

Are there situations in which you can have a dramatic impact? Are there others in which your services are useless? (We'll help you out here: the answer to both questions is YES.)

Acknowledging that you are not the right fit for everyone seems simple, but too often sellers appear to believe that their remedies can cure all of the world's ailments. When you mistakenly think that almost anyone can use what you are promoting, selling becomes an exercise in pushiness or persuasion. Such pressure is a recipe for the traditional sale, aimed at convincing:

> Buyer: I'm not sure that what you are selling will help us.
>
> Seller: *Of course it will help you. It's great! It can help anyone.*
>
> Buyer: I'm still skeptical.
>
> Seller: *Look at the product, the case studies, and the testimonials. Now are you convinced? Here is a pen. Sign right here.*

Convincing is usually adversarial.

Convincing implies that one person is right and the other person just needs to be a bit smarter or better informed. While it is important to believe in what you sell, it is equally important to appreciate where your solution has impact and where it doesn't. When you acknowledge that only some customers are positioned to get the most from your offering, then selling is solving and looking for the right fit.

A posture of solving instead of selling starts before you talk with the prospect. It starts with your internal definition of what business you are in and who your customers are.

Start With What You Do and Whom You Serve

Knowing the unique shapes and designs of your puzzle pieces starts with a few basic questions:

- Whom do you help?
- What do you do to help them?
- Why do they need your help?

These answers may be obvious. For example, a friend of ours provides advisory services (what) to real estate developers (who) when they are building assisted-living homes and evaluating sites to determine if they will attract enough people (why). If you are a pediatric eye doctor or a motorcycle mechanic or are in another highly specialized profession, defining your *who*, *what*, and *why* might be straightforward.

But for many organizations, it is a struggle to create a concise message about *who, what,* and *why.* Companies from start-ups to Fortune 500 organizations often revisit these seemingly simple questions and refine the answers, which can then be combined to form a pithy *elevator pitch*—a summary of your business that you could share with a new acquaintance during the short time before the doors open at the right floor.

The stakes are high for your elevator pitch because, as we illustrated in the last chapter, prospects are likely to classify you—almost instantly—as either 1) someone who is trying to sell them something or 2) someone who may be able to help them solve a problem. Whether your pitch is already polished or seems elusive, we will explain a different way to introduce yourself—a way that's more effective and that sets the stage for Finding Impact Together with highly qualified prospects.

Make a Memorable, Specific First Impression

Your first impression may start with a conversation like this one, a familiar scene at a networking event:

> "Hello, I'm John, the president of Worldwide Inc."
>
> *"Hi, I'm Sue. I'm VP of sales for Universal 123."*
>
> "Oh, what does your company do?"
>
> *"We're a full-service technology and consulting company. Maybe we can help you with something?"*

In that exchange, is John likely to see Sue as someone who is there to solve a problem or as someone who is trying to sell him something? How eager is he to continue the conversation?

Now instead of her "full-service" response, imagine that Sue answers like this:

> *"Companies come to us when they have experienced rapid growth and their technology backbone isn't keeping up. We can help them review where they are, design the right structure, and even help them implement the solution so they can keep focusing on their customers."*

In this second version, is John likely to want to continue talking?

That depends. If he views his company as one that has experienced rapid growth and is behind on technology, he'll probably be highly interested. Otherwise, the conversation may be cut short, but there's still a better chance that he will remember the discussion, and he may even be able to think of a good referral. Meanwhile, Sue can continue to mingle toward a more opportune prospect.

> **Buyer's Perspective:** *If a company defines their offering too broadly, it is less likely that they can help us. We're not looking for generalists in our vendors. We want to hire specific fixers for specific problems.*

The Same Side Pitch

The previous scene contrasts a traditional elevator pitch with our version, which we'll call the Same Side pitch. The traditional elevator pitch presents two basic pieces of information:

- Who we are
- What we do

This line starts with the seller and ends with the seller. The customer may be mentioned in the mix somewhere, but it's pretty much all about the seller. This seller-centric approach will rarely engage the other person, and it may lead straight to the adversarial trap.

The Same Side pitch (like the one Sue used above) starts with the customer's challenge and ends with the customer's success. Let's take a close look at the building blocks.

Pitch Element 1: "Companies come to us when ... "

It is helpful to first help the listener by defining your pool of potential prospects. Do you serve individuals or organizations? If the clients you seek and serve best fit a specific profile, you probably want to put that filter on the table right away. Do you serve government contractors? Parents of high school athletes? Owners of nail salons? Then you might open with,

"Government contractors come to us when ..." or "Parents of high school athletes come to us when ...," and so on.

After homing in on your customers, you arrive at the heart of the Same Side elevator pitch: the customer's challenge. Identify the impetus that brings your prospects to you. Do they need you when they have just lost a key employee? When they are struggling with client attrition? When they need more office space?

As you think about those triggers, remember that the circumstances are far less important than the challenges or problems that ensue. Every "when" can be translated into a "why."

When (Circumstance)	Why (Problem or Challenge)
Just lost a key employee	Because it is understaffed, the company is falling behind on deliveries and facing morale problems.
Struggling with client attrition	The steady loss of clients is eroding profitability and bringing the company's business model into question.
Need more office space	The company cannot take on new work because there is no room for new hires.

Table 2-1: When and Why

Some salespeople resist introducing a problem in their elevator pitch because it seems negative. The thinking is that a *circumstance* is just a fact of life that could happen to anyone (everyone loses a key employee now and then), but a *problem* is messy and embarrassing. Maybe you worry that laying a thorny, stinky problem on the table could repel good prospects who are simply reluctant to acknowledge that they fit the description for the problem you described.

This resistance to a problem-centered pitch is fine... if you're looking for prospects who are in denial and not likely to spend money (sarcasm alert!). The reality is that a problem is much more likely to lead to action than a circumstance is.

Remember the classic advertising proverb that "it's easier to sell aspirin than vitamins." That is, when people are in pain, they are highly motivated to relieve the pain; when people are in generally good health, it is less urgent for them to improve their health incrementally.

That principle applies to your Same Side pitch: the most successful pitch will resonate with the prospect's pain.

What Are Your Prospects Sick and Tired Of?

Where is the customer pain that you can relieve? What are the best words to describe it? These are essential questions in defining your role in the marketplace. Rather than using buzzwords and polished brochure language, the most effective statements of customer pain are often raw and real.

To find those words, start with your best client: the organization for whom you've made the most dramatic impact. What was too much for them to handle without your help? What were they wearily dreading until you took it off their plate with glorious results?

Our friend Bob London of London, Ink, refers to the way customers might describe their own challenges as the *elevator rant*. The elevator rant might occur in an elevator as one executive complains to a colleague, unfiltered:

- "If we could just solve this darned turnover problem!"
- "I'm sick and tired of having these technical failures every other week!"
- "When are we ever going to find a qualified VP of sales—this is killing us!"

The colorful language reflects an important component: *emotion!* When you key into your prospects' passionate complaints and can use them to describe what you do, you will instantly filter prospects down to those who not only need your help, but also know that they need it and are ready to act. We explore this topic more in Chapter 4, which covers urgency and readiness.

Pitch Element 2: "We help them by ... "

The second part of the Same Side elevator pitch explains what you do to help your clients. The good news is that this is the easiest part of the pitch to write. All of us can describe our products and services in great detail.

The bad news is that this is the least important part of the elevator pitch. In fact, too much of the "what" element in a pitch is distracting and can be counterproductive.

Your best prospects are not looking for products and services; they are looking for solutions to problems. They are looking for results. When a salesperson elaborates on features and details without first connecting to a prospect's problem, those words are wasted. How you solve someone's problem is irrelevant if she doesn't think it is a problem or doesn't think you understand it.

Have you ever started a casual conversation with a new acquaintance on an airplane or at a party and had that person start talking about his beloved hobby that you had absolutely no interest in? You keep checking your watch every 15 seconds and saying, "uh-huh," hoping he will stop, but he goes on and on? Remember that feeling when you share what you do in your elevator pitch. Sharing more is far worse if the prospect is not interested.

When a prospect does in fact connect to the problem, he is likely to ask questions. Then you will have the opportunity to share more about what you do and how your genius methods and spectacular results separate you from the pretenders in your field. (We address this more in Chapter 5, Be an Educator.) But before you go deeper into what it is you do, you need to paint a picture of the impact you can have.

Pitch Element 3: "… so they can …"

One of the most widely used and successful sales techniques for diet and fitness products is the set of "before" and "after" pictures. Two simple photos convey a compelling story: an overweight, out-of-shape couch potato with dim prospects uses product X and then becomes healthy, beautiful, and (presumably) successful in all worldly endeavors. *If he can do it, maybe I can do it!*

The Same Side elevator pitch is no more (and no less) than a before-and-after comparison. The prospect needs a clear picture of a problem she relates to, and then a compelling vision of what life will be like after this problem is eliminated. The transformation between the two is the impact of your solution.

The third element of the Same Side elevator pitch is the "after" picture that defines the impact. It is a description of the success that you and your clients share when the work is done.

This success is more than just removing a problem— it includes all of the downstream benefits. Like the problem statement in the first part of the pitch, the results phrase emphasizes impact more than circumstances.

Result	Impact
Help them find the right person	So they can become even more productive than before
Improve service ratings and renewal rates	To reduce their cost of sales and generate more referrals
Get the right space	To inspire their team and lead to optimal productivity and easier recruiting

Table 2-2: Results and Impact

Putting the Same Side Pitch Together

A strong Same Side pitch has a clear and limited explanation of the problem that the seller addresses uniquely and an exciting resolution that will give hope to the right prospects. Here are some examples:

> Old Elevator Pitch 1: "We are a consulting company with experience in procurement. We manage RFPs."

> Same Side Pitch 1: "Companies come to us when they are about to hire a strategic, high-dollar vendor and they want to be sure they don't end up selecting the wrong vendor or paying too much, as they might have in the past."

> Old Elevator Pitch 2: "We are a technology company that provides IT outsourcing services."

Same Side Pitch 2: "Companies come to us when they are sick and tired of investing a ton of money in their IT team and wondering if they are keeping up with technology. We take that off their plates so they can focus on their core business."

Old Elevator Pitch 3: "We are a full-service law firm with offices in Chicago, Washington DC, New York, and London."

Same Side Pitch 3: "Clients come to us when they have struggled to find efficient, sound legal guidance involving multiple major cities or even countries. Our clients value the fact that they can count on skilled local and global resources to protect their interests and avoid or resolve conflicts."

Creating a great Same Side pitch is not easy. It forces sellers to define their value in a very specific manner. This is the power of the pitch, and it's also the greatest challenge because sellers might think that the pitch itself will turn people away.

It will. But a pitch that turns people away is not a bad thing; in fact, it's a strategic necessity that is essential to your success.

Stay Away from Problems You Don't Solve

A puzzle piece is defined by the positive and the negative: where it juts out and where it bends in. Both of these features give it a shape that makes it fit in some places but not others.

The same is true for what you are selling. At a strategic level, it is just as important to know what your company does NOT do as to define what it does. When the boundaries are defined, they should be embraced, not apologized for. Steve

Jobs summed up that idea with the quote "I'm as proud of what we don't do as I am of what we do."

When Scope Outreaches Expertise

Unfortunately, when a client or prospect asks a company to do something outside its area of expertise, the default answer is "Yes, we can do that." Traditional sales training has preached the tenet of selling first and figuring it out later. If a company cannot technically deliver what was requested, then embarrassment and snags ensue. But even when the company can fulfill a request beyond its niche, the expansion in scope tends to weaken the relationship. If you extend into areas beyond your expertise, your client will calculate the average score across each of the categories of service or product you offer. Let's say you offer to help in four areas: two are your core strength, and two are items you could handle but are not your top areas of expertise. If you score 8 out of 10 or your core areas, and 4 out of 10 on the other two, then your average score would be 6. The client would be happy to hire someone who scores an 8, but perhaps not as excited to hire the company they rate a 6.

The following story illustrates how the combination of overreaching and under-delivering often plays out:

> A national association was launching a large new training program for their members. The training was a key pillar of their new strategy, which had been shaped by a trusted consulting firm that had advised the non-profit for years. As the association began to search for a training firm to implement the program, the consulting firm asked to be considered for the work. That resulted in a conversation between Abe, the association director, and Carl, the lead consultant:

Abe: "We didn't know your firm ran training programs."

Carl: "We've got great people here, and they know your organization. We can do it."

After a cursory look at another training company, the association hired the consulting firm to manage and conduct the training program.

Three years later, the results were disappointing. The training initiative had not met its quantitative goals and had received only fair reviews. The consulting firm made several new hires to develop its capability, yet struggled to deliver.

The association concluded that they needed a different partner to run their training program, and the first qualification was extensive experience in training. Worse still, the wasted time and money on the project soured the overall relationship between the consulting firm and the association, and the association terminated the relationship with the consulting firm.

Too often a working relationship evolves from a sweet spot, where the vendor's expertise is perfectly matched to the client's needs, to an overextension. The round peg, which once fit so beautifully, begins to turn square. When a seller says yes too often, trust leads to an outsized scope that ultimately leads to distrust.

To avoid this negative cycle, a seller must be committed to her company's core strengths, and sell only the products and services that deliver the most impact. We explore this further in Chapter 7, Don't Force the Fit.

What's Wrong With Being Opportunistic?

We are not arguing against expansion or trying new things. Nor are we suggesting that every company must limit itself to one and only one defined function. The goal is to create and maintain the level of trust needed for the buyer and seller to have a meaningful collaboration (that is, to stay on the same side).

When a buyer senses that the seller is more interested in selling than in delivering value, trust vanishes and the adversarial mode takes over. In a similar way, a creeping scope can weaken trust as the seller overpromises, then under-delivers.

Companies can be nimble, and they often need to be opportunistic. But responsiveness must be balanced with strategic intent.

Aim to Be "Some Things to the Right People"

A keen awareness of where value can be delivered begins with the sales process. While it seems self-evident that not every company can do everything well, many salespeople go into a meeting trying to be all things to all people.

A posture of universal helpfulness doesn't just set you up for failure; it means less likelihood of making a sale. As the adage states, "When something seems too good to be true, it usually is." When you present a wide list of capabilities as a seller, the discerning buyer begins to discount what you are saying and believes you less. Being all things to all people doesn't ring true and won't sell. Plus, it's exhausting. It's much better and easier to be some things to the right people.

Buyer's Perspective: *It makes me nuts when I see a business website saying "we specialize in" followed by a list of ten or twenty things. Huh? I want to say: "Specialize ... in twenty things?"*

It reminds me of the movie The Princess Bride. The brains behind the devious plot is a character named Vizzini. Each time he is confronted with a potential threat, he says "Inconceivable." Of course, each "inconceivable" scenario is followed shortly by its occurrence. Finally, after the fourth or fifth time Vizzini says "inconceivable" in disbelief, Inigo Montoya says, "You keep using that word. I do not think it means what you think it means." Such is the case with "specialize" when you follow it with a huge list.

One Hundred Pennies of Trust

Imagine that you show up at a sales meeting with a beautiful printed brochure explaining all of your company's services. Your prospect arrives with one hundred "pennies of trust." This money is a resource that she is ready and willing to spend as she listens to you and believes in your capability. But the resource is finite. She cannot get more pennies.

As you share what you do, she puts pennies down on the part of the brochure that describes what you are talking about. Finally, your time is up and her pennies are spent.

How would you like to have those pennies allocated? When the prospect walks out of the meeting, should she have eighty pennies on your main capability and twenty on your secondary capability? Or should there be ten stacks of ten pennies each on different products or services?

This exercise illustrates focus—or perhaps lack of focus. When a company says they do everything well, do you believe them? Do you remember what they do?

Refusing to be Graded on an Average: Five Guys

Perhaps you have had the experience of sitting down at a diner with a menu of over a hundred items, ranging from pizza to soup to fish to gyros. When you ask the server what he recommends, he says: "Everything is great." Hmm. You might conclude that everything can't be great, so each item must be equally mediocre.

Contrast the broad menu offering to Five Guys Burgers and Fries. Five Guys has achieved the unprecedented feat in the restaurant world of simultaneous critical acclaim and spectacular growth. Five Guys is the most reviewed restaurant in the world, and it has grown from one store in Virginia to more than 570 locations in recent years.

The key has been focus. While other restaurants are continually experimenting with new options and menu items, Five Guys has stuck to its limited offering of burgers, hot dogs, and French fries. Five Guys doesn't even sell milkshakes, despite pleas from customers and franchisees to do so.

Owner Jerry Murrell refuses to add to the menu any items that Five Guys cannot be the best at cooking. Why invite mediocre reviews, when your main fare is consistently rated at the very top?

Avoid the Mediocre Reviews

It is exciting when an existing client is willing to pay you to do something more, and it is tempting to present a wide array of solutions to a vast audience of prospects. But remember that you will be graded on any item you add to your menu.

In a client relationship, the evaluation will be based on how you perform. In a sales situation, the grading will be based on how convincingly you present a case that you are qualified to understand and solve a specific problem. Making your case will be easier and more effective when you present the unique understanding and skills that you bring to the world.

When You Think You Are Not Unique

Most people reading this book will not be world-class innovators or acclaimed industry leaders. Some of you are no doubt struggling with the question of how your offering is unique in the marketplace. You may be saying to yourself, "this approach would be great if my job were more unusual, but there are eighteen other (realtors/dentist/accountants/wine stores/gardeners/etc.) within a few miles!"

Take heart. Most of the businesses that Ian works with would not appear to be one-of-a-kind, but they have managed to develop Same Side pitches that set them apart and greatly accelerate their sales process. Even if your profession is well known and you face many competitors with comparable offerings, you still have the opportunity to differentiate and be unique.

In fact, if you are in a profession that is widely understood, you have a great advantage: nearly everyone will understand the core of what you do with little explanation. You don't have to say, "People come to me when they have discomfort in their mouth or teeth; I help them find solutions so they can start eating and sleeping again." You can simply say "I'm a dentist" and they will get it. That's good.

What people won't know is how you are set apart from others in your field. They won't know that you are unique and remarkable. The fact is that you are special, and you specialize.

Convince Yourself First

If you don't believe that your offering is unique, no one else will. So it's worth confirming your specific role in the marketplace, and here's the proof:

When you sell something to a client, it is sold by you. Even if a different company can sell exactly the same product in the same way, it can't be sold by YOU. Ergo, you are unique.

If that last paragraph felt like a mushy moment from a weekend retreat, hang in there. (Trust us, we are not the mushy, weekend-retreat kind of guys.) Embracing your individuality is a legitimate and important part of Same Side Selling. When you connect your unique personality to what and how you sell, it will make your offering more authentic and attractive. Ultimately that will help you sell more and enjoy it more.

Think about your best clients and your favorite experiences. What past projects make you smile when you think about them? Which clients are the most fun to work with? Where have you had the most impact?

It is probable that those clients and projects near the top of your list contain the definition of your uniqueness. When you can articulate the words to describe them, you will be able to find more of them.

Emphasize the Contours That Separate You

As you consider the types of engagements that have been best for you, trends or patterns will emerge. What are the strands that seem to run between your best clients?

Those qualifiers do not necessarily limit the work that you do or represent every client, but they can be useful in defining a specialty that you are known for—or will become known for in the near future.

Your contours might run along one of the following dimensions:

- **Demographic**: There may be demographic qualifiers that separate your best clients. Do they live in a certain geographic region? Are they companies in a specific industry? Does the number of employees or customers they have fall within a certain range? Is there a minimum or maximum revenue amount?
- **Situational**: Your best clients may face similar conditions or circumstances. Are they facing a certain stage of growth? Do they have a common frustration? (Think back to the elevator rant.) Are they experiencing a milestone or common external pressures?
- **Attitudinal**: Do your best clients have certain values? Are there common things that they love? Do they share certain goals? Do they have similar cultures?

Through these dimensions, sellers of everyday products can create their own hill instead of sharing someone else's mountain.

Following are some specific examples of companies we know in mature, competitive fields that have carved out distinctive areas to separate themselves from their competitors. In some cases, they are making themselves distinctive along one dimension; in others, they combine the dimensions.

Industry	Specialty
Fundraising	We specialize in serving faith-based [attitudinal] schools [demographic] with over 300 students [demographic].
Residential real estate	Families with multiple kids in grade school [demographic] come to us when they are looking to live near the best public schools in the region [attitudinal].
Physical therapy	Seniors [demographic] hire me when they are recovering from hip or knee surgeries [situational] and want to regain mobility and get back to competitive sports [attitudinal].
Law	My specialty is serving construction companies [demographic] who are in litigation with their vendors [situational].
Executive coaching	I work with CEOs and VPs [demographic] who are passionate about building innovative cultures where they work [attitudinal].
Financial advising	Our best clients are business owners [demographic] who are planning to exit their company operations within five years [situational].
Recruiting	Clients who love us have more than 100 employees [demographic] and are sick of paying high commission fees to recruiters [attitudinal].
Auto sales	My best prospects are young professionals [demographic] who have done their research and want no-frills, no-nonsense service [attitudinal].

Table 2-3: A Distinctive Offering

From our experience, we suspect that there's a good chance that some of you are still worrying that presenting such a targeted version of your profession will reduce your opportunities. If that is how you feel, we strongly encourage you to simply try it.

It may seem like a paradox: When you are forthcoming about where you don't fit, others around you are more likely to help figure out where you do. Your commitment to making an impact over making the sale is attractive. Finding Impact Together is much better than convincing or being sold.

Put Same Side Selling to Work

We hope you see how you can define your unique position in the marketplace. You first need to convince yourself, and then consider your ideal client's elevator rant to narrow down your best opportunities. Though it may be tempting to expand beyond your strengths, remember that some clients will evaluate you based on your weakest offering, not on your strongest. Define what makes you a great fit. More important, define your boundaries. You might be surprised; telling people where you are not a good fit just might entice them to learn more about your strengths.

- ✔ Where are you essential? Where are you useless?
- ✔ Whom do you serve, and what do you do for them?
- ✔ What are the triggers that cause clients to hire you? Build a When/Why table like Table 2-1 and translate every when into a why. How compelling is the why?
- ✔ Write a draft of your Same Side pitch. Refer to the examples in the Results and Impact table. After you have the draft, call a client and ask them if it sounds right. Use their input to improve the pitch. Repeat.

✔ Write down your core competencies, and note how you would like new prospects to allocate their "hundred pennies of trust." Review the results with the rest of your sales team. Discuss how effectively you are guiding prospects in where they place their pennies.

✔ Is your uniqueness evident in the demographic, situational, or attitudinal qualities of your best clients? If so, identify those specific qualities.

CHAPTER 3
Narrow Your Market

In the previous chapter, we explained how to take inventory of your pieces of the puzzle, so you know which problems you can solve and for whom. The next step is to find someone to build a puzzle with you. In selling, this is where many people lose their way because they underappreciate a key distinction between someone who might be interested in what you sell and someone who is willing to make an investment or willing to change from their existing solution in order to obtain what you sell. Effective selling is a quest to determine whether or not the potential client has an issue worth solving.

Imagine yourself walking down a familiar street, carrying your bag of puzzle pieces. You encounter other people, but some of them are holding board games or decks of cards. These people might be wonderful, but they're not the ones you're looking for; you want to find the ones who have puzzle pieces. Of course, even those people might not have the pieces that complement your pieces. Specifically, you are looking for people who have gaps in their puzzle where your pieces fit perfectly. Your goal in qualifying sales prospects is simple: Find people who not only face problems you can solve, but also recognize those problems and believe they are worth solving.

Knowing which people are worth taking a look at and which ones are not worth your time, today, is essential to your success. The ones who are not a fit—we'll call them non-prospects—pose a great danger to your business because they have the potential to suck in your energy and resources like a black hole. In this chapter, we explain the danger of attempting to serve a wide market, and we present an approach to narrowing your market to the right opportunities. In addition to sharing a specific method for qualifying your prospects, we explain how to use Same Side Selling to have potential buyers qualify themselves.

53

The Cost of Pursuing Too Many Prospects

Many companies spread themselves too thin chasing weak opportunities. This means that when a great opportunity arrives, a company might not have sufficient resources to pursue it properly. When too many prospects are pursued before they are adequately qualified, sales teams expend resources chasing bad deals and pay inadequate attention to the good ones.

Elephant Hunting Can Be Costly

Dave is the CEO of a firm offering outsourced services for bill payment. He was introduced to the controller for a national retailer that had a high level of interest in the outsourced services that Dave's company offers. This retailer also had the potential to become the largest customer of Dave's company. Accordingly, Dave, along with the sales and technical teams, invested many hours in preparing for the first meeting with the retailer and for several subsequent demonstrations.

Unfortunately, the retailer responded slowly and the conversation dragged on for many months. Periods of silence extended for weeks and months, and then the retailer appeared to regain interest. This pattern continued for nearly two years. Finally realizing that the deal was going nowhere, Dave and his team were disgusted with the retailer and mad at themselves for putting so much time and energy into a fruitless lead. When they calculated their investment in travel and employee time on the pursuit, they realized that they had wasted the profit earned from good business in pursuit of a client who was never going to spend money on a solution.

Does that scenario sound familiar? Effort wasted on the wrong prospects is always expensive—not to mention demoralizing. Pursuing large customers is often called "elephant hunting." When you are not able to qualify the opportunity, the pursuit is probably closer to chasing rainbows, and it can be fatal for a business.

In the example above, the seller, Dave, qualified the prospect based on the potential revenue for his company. He thought, "The deal is big enough that we have to chase it." That is a common rationale and it sounds reasonable, but in this case (as in most cases), it proved costly and frustrating.

The Hidden Costs of Playing a Numbers Game

You might say, "So what? Our deals are so large that we can afford to chase ten for every one that we win." Even if your economics do support a high cost of sales and a low conversion rate, failing to narrow your market can hurt your company.

The cost of poor qualifying is more than wasted time. It can take a toll on your team.

Tina is the CEO of a consulting company that relies on project managers to manage proposals. Using project managers to manage proposals seemed to work. Tina asked her project managers to work on proposals in their free time just as the founding team used to do. They would regularly "burn the midnight oil" to bring in clients.

But Tina was starting to hear complaints, which culminated in the heartfelt resignation of their tenth hire. The employee, Sam, said, "I have really enjoyed working here. The team is fantastic. I can live with sacrificing a little time away from my family. I'm happy to put in the effort, but I feel like the time is wasted. In the last twenty proposals, we won three projects. I feel like I spent more time on proposals than we will bill on the projects that we won." Tina realized in that moment that winning just 15 percent of their proposals was not only costing them money, but was also the reason for losing key personnel. She had to find a way to better identify the opportunities worth pursuing. If she didn't, she would struggle to attract and retain top talent.

Even when no one leaves the team, poor qualifying dilutes your resources and can often trigger infighting in organizations. It is common to see salespeople arguing with operational people about which party is to blame when they lose a deal. The flaw is that many organizations play the "numbers game" (you know by now that we're not big fans of playing games in the sales process). They fill up the pipeline with a high quantity of prospects and give insufficient attention to the quality of the prospects.

This is exactly what happened with Tina's company. They chased any potential opportunity without accurately evaluating their potential for success.

The good news is that this unfortunate situation can be turned around. By narrowing their focus and properly qualifying opportunities, Tina's company eliminated half of their pursuits without expending effort and found greater success with the other half. You will probably find a similar upside by improving your qualification process as well. To capture that benefit, though, you might need to revisit how you view the potential outcomes of the selling process.

Embrace the Second-Best Outcome

The numbers-game approach—make enough phone calls, get enough meetings, and you'll find enough business—is based on a disconnect between what sellers think they want and what actually is in their best interests. Take a look at the following scenarios, and rank them from best to worst:

- The initial meeting leads to a follow-up meeting and then results in a sale.
- Immediately after the initial meeting, the client says, "No. This isn't a fit for us."
- The initial meeting leads to a follow-up meeting, and then to two more meetings over a period of months. Finally, the client says that you came in in second place, and they'll consider you in the future.

Everyone would agree that the sale is the most desired outcome. (A sale to the wrong client can be a disaster, however, as we explain in Chapter 7, Don't Force the Fit.)

Which scenario did you select as the second-best outcome?

Instinctively, many people are drawn to the third scenario. With follow-up meetings, the sale seemed to be progressing along the right path. There appeared to be strong interest from the buyer, and the seller's solution *almost* won (at least that is what the buyer implied).

We suggest, however, that the second-best option is the quick "no" (scenario #2). The follow-up meetings in scenario #3 seemed promising, but the net result was no sale and a great deal of additional invested time. If you do not have the fit that will result in a sale where you can make an impact (and get paid), then your best option is to get to "no" as soon as possible.

Protect Your Team: Avoid Silver-Medal Syndrome

Research has shown that silver medalists are less happy than bronze medalists in the Olympics. While the reasons may be different, coming in second is just as undesirable in the business world. In reality, it's often rare that the race is extremely close, with the winning and second-place companies separated by the equivalent of only fractions of a second. Yet in a competitive sales process, the "silver" finisher puts in just as much work as the winner.

Let's take this metaphor a bit further: if you are not going to get a gold medal, you want to be out of the race as soon as possible so you can enter the next contest. Too often, companies fight hard through a long endurance race, only to learn at the end that they never had much of a chance to win.

You can dramatically improve your chances by qualifying your prospects in the right way. Let's turn our attention to the one big thing you need to know to efficiently qualify those prospects.

Qualify by Knowing Why

How do you efficiently attract the right prospects and quickly filter out the wrong ones? The key is to get to why they want your solution. We will explore this step in two parts. In the rest of this chapter, we explain how to get to why as soon as possible. In the next chapter, we will explain how to determine how badly the prospects want what you sell.

Tune in to the Buyer's Challenge

Recall that you must focus on the challenges that your client is facing, instead of focusing on the things you are selling. This principle is true at every step of the selling process.

> **Buyer's Perspective:** *Salespeople have been trained to ask for need, budget, and authority. The good ones ask questions about the important problems that need to be solved and about ways we can measure success together.*

In *To Sell is Human*, Daniel Pink explains the concept of "attunement." Attunement is being highly aware of the customer's viewpoint and always having that at the forefront of your mind. To successfully qualify a potential buyer, you must be attuned with the person. The sooner you tune in to the prospect's perspective, the more efficient the sales process will be.

Too often, salespeople aim to bring buyers over to their own point of view. They drown prospects with a fire-hose of information in the form of lengthy spiels, glossy brochures, and slick, animation-filled slide presentations. Old-school sellers figured that qualifying prospects meant showing them everything and then saying, "Are you interested?"

You can move ahead of the competition with effective attunement. Ask yourself, "What would be important to me if I were in their shoes? What would I want to know before I made a purchase?" Most important, ask yourself, "Why would the prospect need what I am selling?"

Know the Most Important Buyer Questions

Ian has led more than five hundred CEOs through the exercise below, and the results show an interesting pattern in how executives make purchasing decisions. The exercise starts with the following scenario:

> Someone on your team comes to you to buy a service for $20,000. What questions would you have to ask your employee to determine whether you want to make that purchase or save your resources for another purpose?

Working in groups, the executives have to come up with a list of questions they would need answered in order to make an informed decision about buying a fictitious service called the Gazertenblatt service (we told you it was fictitious).

> It costs $20,000, it requires no resources on your part, and the company guarantees that you won't need the service for another ten years or you get your money back. They are not the only company that offers the service, but their clients tell them that they are the best.

The first assignment for the executives is to develop five questions they would need answered in order to make an informed buying decision. *Take a moment to think through that process and formulate your own five questions before continuing.*

The executives are then asked to narrow the list to three questions. *After you have narrowed your list down to three questions, continue reading.*

The common questions are almost the same across industries, genders, and company sizes. The three questions needed to make an informed decision come down to:

1. What problem needs to be solved?
2. What are the likely results if we buy this service?
3. Why should we buy it from this company?

An interesting pattern has emerged: In most groups, the first question written down is "What is it?" However, when narrowing the list of questions, participants realize that knowing what the service is has little meaning compared to knowing why they need it. As one CEO explained, "If I know the problem it solves and my likely outcome, I don't really care what you are doing or how you do it." In other words, **why** bumps **what** off the list.

Your list might have contained other valid questions: questions about risks, guarantees, or references. Those questions roll up under the topic of "likely results." Buyers ask about references and risks to gain confidence that a seller can actually deliver as promised.

But the main takeaway turns much of accepted marketing on its head. Sales literature and discussions that center on the product are missing what is most important. Instead of trumpeting what you sell, your best starting point is a solid understanding of why a buyer would be interested.

Get on the Fast Track to Why

In the previous chapter, we presented an effective method of presenting a problem and solution in your Same Side pitch. Now we are going to show you the next level in presenting that pitch.

You Probably Won't Be Able to Help Them

Let's say you have a meeting with a potential client. Minutes before you arrive, someone asks that executive, "I see a meeting on your calendar. What is it about?" She can give one of two answers: 1) "Someone is coming to try to sell us something"; or 2) "We have this issue we are facing, and we have asked this person to meet with us to see if he can help." Our preferred answer, of course, is the latter. But even if the prospect sees you more as a seller than as a solver, you have the ability to pull the situation out of the adversarial trap within the first three minutes of your meeting and set a completely different tone for the conversation.

To get (or stay) on the same side, we will build on the understanding that you are not the best fit for every potential client (nor is every prospect a good fit for you). It will help us to be more specific on the second point, so let's ask a specific question: Of all the people you meet, what percentage of them are likely to become paying customers in the short term?

Either write down the number or just think of it. In Ian's experience, having posed this question to over a thousand executives, sellers universally recognize that they are likely to do business with less than half of the people they encounter. Most sellers, in fact, say the number is less than 5 percent, but nearly everyone (maybe you, too) agrees that the number is less than 50 percent.

Entice, Disarm, Discover

Whatever your number is, it shouldn't depress you. In fact, we are going to use it as part of a highly effective tactic to quickly qualify a prospect. The formula is:

Entice	Entice the customer by identifying something you have that might be of interest.
Disarm	Make it clear that you are not there to sell, but want merely to see if there is a fit.
Discover	Trigger a discovery phase in which you learn about them (instead of spending a meeting talking about your stuff).

Any three-step formula might sound overly simplistic, so it's OK if you have an instinctive resistance to Entice, Disarm, Discover. But this approach is worth pursuing because it will almost certainly accelerate your efforts in Finding Impact Together. We'll illustrate with one of Ian's clients, a benefits insurance broker called Potomac Companies, Inc.

The Same Side pitch for Potomac Companies starts with their typical client's elevator rant (we covered elevator rants in Chapter 2): "We hate the trend of our healthcare costs' growing from $1 million to $2 million over the next seven years. We'd rather have that money for other things." Potomac Companies' formula to Entice, Disarm, and Discover sounds like this:

> **[Entice]** We work with clients who are currently spending $1 million on insurance benefits and who realize that if costs are left unchecked, that number will grow to $2 million over the next seven years. At that point, clients will have spent an additional $3.5 million. They tell us they have other things they'd rather do with that money. For the right clients, we can help them reduce their future healthcare costs.

> **[Disarm]** *We find that we can have a dramatic impact on less than half of the organizations we meet with about this issue.* But if addressing those cost increases is important to you,

> **[Discover]** we'd be happy to speak with you to learn more about your situation to see if we can help.

Potomac Companies found that using this formula early in a sales meeting had a palpable impact on the conversation. The difference-maker was the Disarm step: it seemed that as soon as the Potomac reps mentioned that they could help only half of the companies they met with, the prospect appeared eager to be among that fortunate group. In some cases, the prospects began to convince the seller, presenting a passionate case for why they were positioned to benefit from Potomac's solutions.

This situation seems like a flip of the usual selling dynamic, and it is. But Entice, Disarm, Discover is not a manipulative Jedi mind trick. It is based entirely on integrity and reality. Potomac Companies tracks the progress of each client and finds they can actually have a dramatic impact for about half of the companies with whom they meet. They even provide a scorecard that illustrates where they believe they could have the greatest impact. This combination of awareness and openness demonstrates to the client that Potomac is focused on solving the client's issues and delivering results. Acknowledging that they might not be able to help the prospect takes Potomac Companies out of the category of "someone trying to sell something" and puts them on the same side as the buyer.

Let Buyers Qualify Themselves

Perhaps the quickest path to the adversarial trap is presumption: the belief that the seller knows the buyer's situation and the right solution. When sellers focus only on what they are selling, this presumption might not even be perceived as a problem. When the emphasis shifts to why buyers would buy, their circumstances and rationale become more important, and the seller needs to qualify the buyer to ensure a good fit.

But the common practice of qualifying leads or prospects implies that the *seller* has to make the judgment of fit. In the Disarm component described above, the seller plainly states that his organization can't help everyone, and implies that they might well not be able to help the prospect. While that candor builds trust, it also does something more important: it shifts the burden of qualifying to the buyer.

In fact, the easiest way to qualify customers is to let them do it for you. That's right: let the buyers qualify themselves. We will share two approaches. One allows potential clients to evaluate their situation. The other falls into a category called assignment selling.

Self-Evaluation

One of Ian's clients was being inundated with demonstration requests from potential customers. Ian's client was expending considerable resources preparing demos for people who had no justifiable reason to make a purchase, but were mostly curious to see the client's advanced technology. Working with Ian, the client developed a list of conditions that would warrant an investment in what he was selling. On the website was a link that said, "See if we are a potential fit." The resulting Web page said, "Our technology is not a fit for everyone. But if you are experiencing at least three of the following seven challenges, then we might be able to help," and presented a list of the seven conditions.

The result might surprise you. Nearly all of the requests came from people who clearly faced two of the issues and were emphatic about convincing the seller (and themselves) that they also had a third one. The result is that Ian's client ended up spending less time preparing demos and closed a much higher percentage of opportunities than in the past. Potential buyers would call and say, "We definitely face two of the issues, and we think that we have enough parts of other ones to count as a third one."

Assignment Selling

Marcus Sheridan of TheSalesLion.com describes a process called "assignment selling." Marcus discovered, from his Internet traffic analysis, that if a prospect read thirty articles on his company's website, that prospect was extremely likely to become a customer. There seemed to be a clear path to more efficient selling: getting all prospects to read thirty articles. But how could Marcus get his prospects to read that much? The answer was simple: he gave them homework.

Marcus created an ebook that consisted of thirty articles. He made a practice of informing every potential customer, "I want to ensure that you are well informed in making this decision, so I am sending you this ebook to read prior to our meeting on Friday. I'll call you first thing Friday morning to check that you have had time to read it. If you haven't, we can reschedule."

If the customer had not read the ebook, then Marcus, true to his word, would reschedule. In his industry, the success rate for in-home meetings is about 15 percent. Marcus's company enjoys a success rate of over 80 percent.

Assignment selling can take many forms, in addition to required reading. The assignment can be to complete a self-assessment form or simply to list the most important buying criteria.

Put Same Side Selling to Work

Chasing too many prospects is exhausting and costly. One of the most important conditions for growth is to prune the wrong investments and focus on the opportunities where you are positioned to win and to deliver impact. To qualify those prospects, you must subordinate what you are selling and bring the prospects' reasons for buying—the why—to the forefront. As the seller, you cannot presume to be the expert on why buyers buy. The buyers themselves are better suited to qualify themselves. As you shift the burden of qualification to the buyers through self-evaluation or assignment-based selling, your work as the seller decreases. At the same time, you solidify your position as someone who is there to solve a problem (and not just sell something).

✔ Ensure that every discussion helps the client organization discover a) the problem you solve that makes them need what you offer; b) the likely outcome of your solution with respect to that problem; and c) why you are the best option for their current situation.

✔ Make a list of marketing content items that would allow prospective clients to perform self-evaluations. (These items could be surveys, diagnostics, or articles such as "The Five Most Important Things to Consider Before Buying.") Do you have these content items available? If not, plan to create and publish them in the next quarter.

✔ Develop a scorecard to allow you and the buyer to evaluate, from the same side of the table, the potential impact you can have on the client's company. Remember that acknowledging that you cannot have a dramatic impact today will increase the likelihood of the buyer's considering you in the future.

✔ Write your version of Entice, Disarm, and Discover. Try it out on friends or colleagues by saying, "I think this might be a better way for me to introduce our services," and see what they think.

CHAPTER 4
Get to the Truth

Here's a quick recap of the first part of the book: you're solving a puzzle and you know your unique offering. You are focusing on why a buyer is buying, instead of on what you are selling. Now as we move forward, we need to recognize that the knowledge of *why*—while essential—is incomplete. There is more truth to uncover that is directly related to when and if the buyer will actually buy, as well as whether the buyer's organization is positioned to benefit from your solution.

In this chapter we focus on two factors that drive when a buyer will be ready to spend money for your solution: urgency and readiness. Urgency is the perceived immediate impact on the problem that you would solve. Readiness is the buyer's ability to realize a benefit from the solution you offer.

Failing to get to the truth increases risk: the risk of spending too much energy on the wrong prospect, the risk of losing the sale because of insufficient understanding, and the risk of selling into a situation where you are not positioned to have a positive impact. These risks often lead to regrets like these:

> "Why did we spend so much time educating them when they didn't end up buying anything?"

> "They were polite and interested, but they never pulled the trigger."

> "They had too much other stuff going on to give our project the attention it needed, and now they're unhappy because they are not seeing results."

Getting to the truth in the course of selling is sometimes referred to as "discovery" or "consultative selling." It is commonly practiced in the sale of high-dollar, high-complexity services and is seen as a way to build buy-in and to connect to the buyer's pain.

But even for less complex products, Same Side Selling requires getting to the truth about the buyer's situation. We think of this step as turning all of the puzzle pieces right-side up. After all, who would try to solve a puzzle with the pieces upside down?

The Need for a Good Diagnosis

You can think of the process of turning pieces right-side up as a diagnosis. This step protects your resources (time, energy, and money) and can help set you apart in the marketplace.

Diagnose to Protect Your Investment

In game-based selling, getting to the truth may be optional. After all, once the buyer shows a willingness to buy, all that matters is closing the deal. You sell, you win, game over: the impact of your solution is secondary.

But when you are focused on *solving, not selling*, you must uncover the relevant details of the buyer's situation. Those details will reveal the extent to which you can have an impact, and they will inform your decision on whether to pursue the opportunity.

Remember that your puzzle pieces don't fit just anywhere. Where they do fit, they complete the picture and everyone benefits. To find those fits as often as possible, you must qualify prospects and opportunities and flee those that are not a good fit.

This is worth repeating: you will limit your impact unless you actively qualify your opportunities. Your resources are best spent in situations that meet all three of the following criteria:

1. The issue your client faces has sufficient impact on her organization to warrant an investment or change to solve the problem.
2. You have a dialogue with the stakeholders to understand their underlying issues—and to confirm that they know that you understand their situation.
3. You bring capabilities or offerings that make you better suited than others to solve the client's problem.

In between discussing the problem (step 1) and identifying a solution (step 3) is the important step of diagnosis. It is to your benefit to advance the diagnosis discussion, early and intentionally.

In Chapter 3 we revealed how a second-place finish can actually be the worst outcome, because you expend the energy to pursue a customer but miss out on the reward. Unfortunately, you can end up in second place even when you appear to have no other competitors. How? By losing to the buyer's status quo. This outcome happens when the so-called buyer evaluates alternatives, decides to buy nothing, and stays with his current solution. Doing nothing is just as much of a decision as selecting another vendor. Rightly or wrongly, the buyer concludes that the impact of a new solution is not significant enough to justify making a change. When you lose to the status quo, it can feel like you ran your heart out, only to learn that the race didn't count.

Early in the life of one of Ian's prior companies, Ian was pursuing an opportunity at a large pharmaceutical company. The prospect had seen a demonstration of the company's software and wanted to arrange an on-site demonstration for other members of his team. As Ian probed to uncover the other parties involved, the prospect said, "You don't need to worry about that. I know what we need, and we have fifteen people who are all looking forward to your visit next Thursday." Instead of pushing back, Ian agreed to have the meeting. (Spoiler alert: that's the last time Ian would agree to such a meeting under those conditions.) The meeting appeared to go well, but there was no immediate follow-up. Every week or so, Ian would ask the prospect, "Have you made a decision yet?" After six months, the company decided that they were going to abandon the project. The prospect explained, "Your technology was very good, but we realize that we can live with what we have."

Ian had assumed that when the prospect saw his product demonstration, his company would fall in love with the solution. Though the company may have been impressed with the solution, they had no sense of urgency to solve their problem and move the investment forward.

To ensure that your efforts are well spent, you need to become an expert at getting to the truth with the buyer. After you learn why a buyer would need your solution, the next question is whether the buyer considers the issue worth solving. When Ian moved forward without ensuring that the client knew the impact of the problem, he took a risk. Had he pushed back and asked more questions before providing a demonstration, it would have seemed to slow down the momentum of a prospect eager to see a product. In fact, hindsight teaches us that asking questions would have saved Ian time and effort. It might even have provoked a discussion that showed the people at that company that their issue was more important than they realized.

Diagnose for a Competitive Advantage (for the Right Customers)

Getting to the truth in a diagnosis will help you protect your investment. It is also a meaningful way to set your company apart from others. More often than not, the buyer will buy from the seller that she believe best understands her situation. That perceived understanding will outweigh price, features, and experience.

Buyers believe that you understand their situation when you are proficient at walking them from the symptom (the statement of their issue) to the diagnosis (what impact the issue has on their organization and how important it is for them to solve it, compared to other things on their plate).

While good diagnostic skills will help you attract more customers, it is important to stress that this is not a tactic of persuasion or manipulation. A diagnosis is a means to get to the truth. The truth is always your ally in Same Side Selling, even when it seems to decrease the likelihood of making a sale.

> **Buyer's Perspective:** We can tell when the so-called diagnostic process is simply checking the box, because the salesperson isn't really listening, and all answers seem to lead to their solution. How convenient!

As you investigate the prospect's needs, listen and learn before you prescribe. If you do not have the skills or resources to provide the best solution, don't try to fake it. Recognize that your client will probably notice the mismatch, quite possibly from your body language and tone. If anything, you want to acknowledge the lack of fit before the buyer does. This acknowledgment will help to build trust and may change the tone of the conversation (in a way that's similar to the Disarm phase described in Chapter 3). If you are comfortable identifying your gaps, then buyers are more likely to believe you when you present your strengths.

A bad fit is not a bad thing. Finding that your solution will not dramatically help the prospect is a successful outcome for getting to the truth. While it may close a window of opportunity, it will keep the relationship door open for the future. You will discover in Chapter 7, Don't Force the Fit, that getting to a quick "no" often means that you'll be welcomed back whenever you want.

Diagnose Like the Professionals

Fortunately, all of us have seen diagnosis modeled well. The field of medicine illustrates the importance of uncovering the meaningful details of a patient's symptoms, as well as sound tactics to get to the truth. Imagine the following scenarios:

> You visit a doctor and say that your elbow hurts. The physician looks at you and says, "Yep—It's tennis elbow. I'll schedule you for surgery tomorrow." Would you feel confident in that course of action? Or would you run from the office, never to come back?

> You call your doctor because you have a stuffy nose. You ask the doctor to prescribe an antibiotic. The physician responds by saying, "I'm not sure that you have a bacterial infection. If you don't, the antibiotic will not help and could hurt. Can we do some diagnosis first to ensure that I recommend the proper treatment?"

Jumping to a solution before knowing the key facts is bad medicine, whether it's the patient or the doctor who makes the assumption. Good doctors earn trust by collaboratively diagnosing the patient's situation. They ask questions like "How long has this been going on? What have you tried to alleviate the pain? Is it affecting your day-to-day life? Does it wake you up at night?"

The same types of diagnostic questions help you get to the truth about your prospect. Knowing this truth is necessary before you prescribe a remedy. We love the medical metaphor because it not only helps with the process, but also reveals the intent. Same Side Selling is about getting to the truth as quickly as possible.

Get to the Truth about Urgency

No matter what you are selling, your success will largely be driven by the buyer's sense of urgency. Urgency makes the difference between a prospect who only understands the value you provide and one who is also ready to act to capture that value.

Interest doesn't lead to sales; *urgency* does. As a rule, the buyer should have at least at much urgency as the seller. If you have a greater sense of urgency to solve the problem than your prospect does, then you should be prepared to pay for it because the prospect will not.

Don't Create False Urgency

When the seller is more committed to fixing the problem than the buyer is, you can easily fall into the adversarial trap. It's easy to get stuck convincing rather than solving, and you can come across as desperate and alarmist.

Picture a home-security-system salesman trying to make a sale to a resident who believes his neighborhood is safe, or a life insurance salesman painting a picture of how "accidents can happen" to a reluctant prospect. Your field of business might not evoke the same visceral reaction, but when you are trying to persuade someone that his problem is bigger than he is ready to acknowledge, you risk a perception of fear-mongering.

Buyer's Perspective: *Why is this person trying to magnify the problem and make it sound so bad? She's trying to scare me so I'll buy what she's selling. I'm not going to fall for that.*

You may bring passion to what you sell and appreciate how it can make a difference. But your urgency as the seller is not enough to propel the sale. If you press forward even when your prospects do not perceive a problem worth solving, you will build a reputation as someone who is always trying to sell, not solve.

At the same time, prospects do not always wear their urgency on their sleeve. They might need your help to realize the full impact of their problem before they feel the appropriate level of urgency. You can help them discover the impact and importance of their issue.

Assess Urgency with Issue, Impact, and Importance

Traditional lead qualification centers on budget, authority, and need. Some organizations also track the buyer's timeline to make the acronym "BANT." While this mnemonic can be helpful, focusing on BANT reveals only indirect indicators of why a buyer would buy. Budgets and timelines often change.

In today's world, with more decisions being made through consensus, authority can be misleading or ambiguous.

A simpler and more predictive path to qualify urgency is to uncover the buyer's issue, impact, and importance:

- **Issue:** What problem is the client organization trying to overcome, or what is their goal?
- **Impact:** What happens if they don't solve the problem? What downstream problems is it causing?
- **Importance:** Compared to other things on the client's plate, how important is this?

This framework provides a strong indicator of urgency and is a shortcut to Finding Impact Together. Finding enough impact will lead the client to finding unbudgeted dollars. Let's walk through the steps of determining the issue, impact, and importance.

Define the Issue

When you identify why the buyer will buy, you can define the issue his company has. This is usually the easy part, as your customer may draw from a short list of possible problems.

For example, if you are selling information technology (IT) services, your potential buyer might have an interest in his company's systems being more reliable, so he is contemplating outsourcing IT support to you.

Define the Impact

The impact shows how the issue is hurting the prospect's company or holding them back. Defining the impact can start with a list of problems related to the issue. This is where good questions and even better listening are essential, because impacts can vary widely for your prospects.

Imagine that you are selling marketing services to a prospect, and you have determined that the company's issue is the lack of a single compelling advertising message. The potential impacts from that issue cover a wide range:

- Disappointing sales
- Confusion in the marketplace
- Low morale because the staff is not proud of their message
- Higher costs to get multiple messages out

The impact includes all the problems that the issue implies. In fact, "implication" is a helpful word to remember when defining the impact of a client's problem. "Implication" is the "I" in Neil Rackham's sales classic, *SPIN Selling* (MacGraw-Hill, 1988). In the book, Rackham explains that prospects often need to be guided through implications to understand "the seriousness of the problem." You can guide a buyer through that thought process by using open-ended questions about impact:

> "You said the lack of a single marketing message is a problem. How is that affecting your company?"

> "Is this causing any other problems, or is it pretty well contained?"

> "Does this issue affect your sales in any way? Your operations? Your profitability?"

Define the Importance

Finally—and critically—you need to evaluate the importance of the buyer's problem. Your prospects may be able to pick their issue from a short list. Their impact is an essay question, in which they describe the downstream problems. Importance is always a relative matter and is best assessed using a numeric scale.

The best question for gauging importance is, "Compared to other things on your plate, how important is this one on a scale of 1 to 10?" The answer to this question will provide great insight into the sense of urgency and is the quickest way to see if you are making progress toward a solution or wasting time.

If They Don't Really Care, They Are Not Prospects

If you find that more than half of the prospects you talk to are committed to solving the problem that you address, then you are doing a fine job of qualifying. Sellers tend to believe that if they can just get in front of the right person, they will be able to speak to a problem that the prospect cares about.

Unfortunately, just because prospects are meeting with you doesn't mean they care. We hate to break it to you, but we'd hate even more to see you waste time with non-prospects. Even when they admit to having a problem that you address, that does not, by a long shot, ensure that they are committed to solving it.

Don't Convince Them; Let Them Convince You

Your best opportunities occur when clients convince you that their problems are worth fixing. This idea is similar to the concept of having buyers qualify themselves, which we explained in the last chapter. In the adversarial trap, the burden of establishing importance falls on the seller alone. This is not the case when you are using Same Side Selling.

We are not minimizing the importance of helping clients identify the impact of the issues they face. But after that conversation, the process comes back to defining importance: "Now that we have taken a look at the impact, how important is it for you to address this issue?" On a scale of 1 to 10—where 10 is the greatest importance—your true prospects will rate their importance at 8 or higher. Rarely do potential buyers decide to make a change or investment when the response is below an 8.

When the Importance Just Spills Out

In fact, after a good discussion of impact, you might not even need to ask how important a problem is. It might simply spill out: "I can't tolerate this problem anymore—who can help me solve it? If anyone has a solution, please share it with me because I need this thing FIXED!"

Does that sound like an 8, a 9, or a 10?

When a prospect clearly identifies an issue, understands the full impact, and then rates the importance high, selling becomes easy. In fact, it's not really selling; it is solving.

The buyer's urgency is an essential qualifier, and assessing it should be part of any formal sales process. Many sales organizations monitor every potential opportunity in their "pipelines" or "funnels." As you look at your open leads, consider recognizing only those opportunities where you can define the prospect's issue, impact, and importance. Would the urgency justify the change or investment? If not, does this opportunity really belong in your pipeline?

Have the Right Conversation

We have presented the issue/impact/importance (I-3) model as a way to guide your conversation with a prospect. The framework is immensely helpful, but it does not work well as a checklist or worksheet that you hand to a prospect. Finding impact happens in the context of a relationship. Questions and discussions are your best tools to get to the truth.

Just as in a conversation with a friend, each question needs to relate to the prior answer. If you simply jump from question to question without acknowledging the other person's responses, then you'll sound like you are pursuing your own agenda (and get perilously close to the adversarial trap!). The answers about the issue, its impact, and its importance might emerge in a different order or be intertwined.

Remember, your goal is simply to Find Impact Together (FIT). You don't need to convince anyone, promote yourself, or defend your solution. It's not about your solution; it's about the client's problem. This posture allows the seller to stop thinking about selling and simply listen and learn.

Same Side Questions and Answers

The goal of every conversation is the chapter title: *get to the truth.* While we will refer to our overall mantra of Finding Impact Together, it's possible that you may conclude that the prospect's issue is not significant enough to solve at this time. Consider these questions and possible responses:

- "I want to be sure that we don't miss anything important. Can you please share what sparked you to pursue this project?"

* **Weak answer:** "We're just trying to do some research on our options for the future." (The prospect lacks urgency.)

* **Strong answer:** "We all of a sudden realized that this issue is costing us $X per quarter. If we don't find a solution quickly, I'm going to be looking for a new job." (Here we have a clearly defined I-3.)

* **Adversarial alert:** "Why do you need to know that? Can't you just give us the price?" (Behold the adversarial trap in full regalia.)

- "Let's say you don't solve the issue; is it just a nuisance? How is the organization affected by it?"

  * **Weak answer:** "I don't know that there is any real impact. But we'd like to find a solution." (Demonstrating a lack of clarity, the client assumes that he'll get approval because he wants it.)

  * **Strong answer:** "Nuisance? Only if $2 million of loss is a nuisance. This is our top priority." (Here's another clearly defined I-3.)

  * **Adversarial alert:** "The impact has a direct connection to your price. At this point, you guys need to sharpen your pencils or we are going to have to go with another vendor." (Prepare for the adversarial trap onslaught—this prospect has already focused on price over value.)

- "How will we be able to measure success? If we can't do it, we want to get out of your way."

* **Weak answer:** "Everyone is on board with this. We don't need to worry about metrics. Just get it done." (A vague impact statement often leads to long delays or to decisions that favor the status quo.)

* **Strong answer:** "We should be able to see an improvement of x percent within six months. Is that reasonable?" (They know exactly how to measure success, and they are circling back with you to make sure you can deliver.)

* **Adversarial alert:** "We'll worry about that. Just get us the proposal." (They don't see you as being on the same side of the table with them.)

These questions all center on the buyer's perspective, not the seller's. Do not try to persuade your client to give a specific answer. Rather, uncover the truth. Take a look at these examples and develop your own questions. Then consider what would constitute strong, weak, and adversarial responses to your questions. This way, when you ask the questions and get responses, you'll be prepared to interpret them.

What If They Just Don't Know the Impact?

There are times when clients know they want to fix something, but don't recognize the impact that "something" is having on their business. One of the best ways to help them discover the impact is through third-party stories (which we will explain further in Chapter 5, Be an Educator). Those brief stories might sound like this:

"Our other clients in your field tell us that XYZ is a big issue because it affects their compliance fines. How common is that?"

"We were speaking with another client who shared that the XYZ issue cuts their production by more than 20 percent. How do you address that?"

"Another organization like yours said that by fixing XYZ, they could drive another 15 percent to their bottom line. How realistic is that?"

In each case, notice that you are not asking yes/no questions. Rather, you ask open-ended questions to invite thoughtful responses.

Common Questions to Avoid

Do you use the following questions in your sales qualification process? We call attention to these questions because they often lead directly to the adversarial trap.

"Who is the decision maker?"

This question will almost always produce the same answer regardless of the facts: "I am." The question can make the other party feel uncomfortable. Are you asking to cut this person out of the process and get to the "decision maker"?

Instead, consider asking, "When you made decisions like this in the past, who else got involved?" This question taps into the person's experience. You can even follow up with "How do you envision this process differing from the last time?"

"What is your budget?"

When you ask this question, what are you hoping to learn?

Buyer's Perspective: *When you ask "What's your budget," I'm thinking "Whatever I tell them, they are going to give me a price that is 99.8% of that number."*

The moment you ask the budget question, the buyer starts guarding his wallet. At that moment, you are focused on how much money the prospect has to buy your product or service, not on the issue, impact, and importance. This approach triggers an adversarial trap in which you are focused on the sale, not the result. Instead of asking about budget, remember to focus on FIT—Finding Impact Together. Once you and the client realize the impact of the issue, you'll be able to determine the value of the solution.

The Budget Trap

Asking about the budget may seem like a good idea, but what if the prospect's number is too low? What if the budget is double what your solution might cost? Have you ever won a deal that never happened because the client's budget went away? Have you ever landed an account when the company did not have a budget, but found the money because the issue was important enough? Instead of asking about budget, keep Finding Impact Together.

Their Readiness Is Your Concern

When your prospects lack urgency, you may be in for a long wait before they sign the contract. But even when clients are eager to sign your contract, it is still critical to get to the truth about their *readiness* to adopt your solution.

Again we point to the contrast between the Always Be Closing mentality and Finding Impact Together. If your ultimate goal is to sell, then the buyer's ability to benefit from your sale is simply his responsibility. But if you are *solving, not selling,* then the client's readiness is very much in your interest. And you should not move forward until you know that the client can implement your offering to achieve the desired results.

Your interest in how the client company is positioned to use what you sell them is not purely selfless. Implementation problems can cause other, long-term problems, especially when you're delivering services. Perhaps you've learned that lesson the hard way, as Jack did years ago:

> Our invoice processing firm brought in a national software company on a large contract, and we were all excited to get started. The implementation was bumpy from the beginning, because the client did not have the centralized operations that we expected and relied on. We ended up helping the client make the needed changes, but that was really outside of our expertise. After months of delay, the client was extremely disappointed that the savings we targeted were not materializing. It truly was not our fault—we just couldn't get our solution in place because the client was not ready.

Part of the truth you must uncover while qualifying your prospects is about whether they can take advantage of your solution. When this readiness depends on specific factors, they must be identified. When buyers fail to get results, they will often feel that the seller let them down—even if the failure is the buyer's fault.

Stakeholders and Structure

The sale itself is not the finish line. (We will expand on this in Chapter 9, Deliver Impact.) To ensure that your prospect's organization can enjoy the impact from your solution, what tools or processes must they have in place? When you think back on some of your spectacular client success stories, you can probably identify factors that expedited success. With the failures, those key factors may have been missing.

Depending on what you sell, the cause of a failure may be technical, organizational, or political. It is important to note that your main contact during the sales process might not be the person directly affected by the solution. He might not have the answers you seek. In that case, you need to ensure clear communication with the stakeholders. Failure to do so is analogous to playing a game of telephone. The lead buyer communicates his needs to someone on his team, who passes it along to someone else. Eventually an answer gets back to you, but it might lack the definitive clarity you need. This situation is a recipe for failure.

To engage others in the process, try asking questions like:

> "In our experience, if we don't get stakeholders involved to explain the underlying issues up front, we run the risk of delivering the wrong solution, which makes us all look bad. I'd hate to put either of us in that situation. What's the best way for us to include them in a way that's comfortable for you?"

Notice that in this example, we illustrate how perilous it is for both buyer and seller if the right people are not included. Note also that we avoid asking for the "decision maker," but still reach for the people with authority.

> "Who else is affected by this project? How can we engage them in a way that works for you?"

In this example, we ask who else is affected, and then—to signal our intent to work together—ask how "we can engage them in a way that works for you." With this approach, you respect the position of your direct contact and indicate that together you'll include others.

Bringing additional people into the effort of getting to the truth is likely to slow down the sales process in the short run, but this step is an investment that will save you time and pain later. A little extra work and care up front will put you and the customer on the same side of the table so you can solve the customer's problem.

Clarity on the Shape of the Solution

We want to address a specific area where failure to get to the truth can cause great pain for service providers: outsourcing. In recent years, companies have turned to the marketplace to provide functionality that was traditionally handled in-house. This change provides more opportunities for sellers to serve, but also more potential for overlaps or conflicts with the internal capability of their customers.

It is critical that the client understands where the offered solution starts and stops before the sale is made. Consider what happens if a solution purchase is made when the buyer's organization doesn't really know the size and shape of their puzzle pieces—that is, they don't know their own capabilities well enough to understand how the seller's solution will fit in. How will that situation play out? In one of three ways:

- **The gap:** The buyer overestimates his organization's capability and coverage, so the solution bought doesn't meet the needs that the buyer expects and leaves part of the problem unsolved.
- **The overlap:** The buyer underestimates his organization's capability, so pieces overlap and the seller ends up fighting to implement parts of a solution that the buyer doesn't really need.
- **The miracle:** You get really, really lucky and things just happen to fit.

If you're selling a simple solution (maybe a twenty-piece puzzle?), you have greater odds of catching the miracle. But even then, it's better not to leave it to chance. How will the buyer react if you slow down the sale and persuade him to take a closer look at his company's needs?

When They Won't Answer Your Questions

As noted previously, having open conversations begins with the tone of your first interaction. If your contact is holding back, you may have sounded like someone trying to sell something instead of like someone solving a problem.

It's also possible that you presented everything in the best way, and the prospect is still reluctant to share. As context, remember that many buyers have been conditioned to expect the adversarial trap, and they may fear being burned in some way because of prior experiences. Or there may be political reasons that someone on the buying team is uncooperative. Then again, you may have just come across a less-than-pleasant personality.

No matter the reason, the inability to adequately assess urgency or readiness should be a warning sign. If the Same Side approach and the tactics presented in this chapter don't help you get to the truth, you might need to reconsider the opportunity. For most of us, poor communication will limit our impact and is one reason that pieces don't fit together.

You need to get to the truth.

Put Same Side Selling to Work

After understanding why a buyer would buy, the seller needs to assess the buyer's urgency and readiness. These two factors determine when prospects will become paying customers and whether they are able to truly adopt and benefit from the seller's solution. The medical diagnosis model is a great tool for getting to the truth with a buyer, and using the issue/impact/importance framework will reveal the buyer's urgency.

- ✔ Does your standard sales process include a diagnostic step? If not, do you think you should add one? If so, how well do you perform the diagnosis?
- ✔ Think of a specific selling situation in which your urgency as the seller outweighed the buyer's urgency. Talk to someone on your team about the situation, describing the context and how it felt.
- ✔ Identify three of your most promising sales opportunities. For each one, write out the issue, impact, and importance as you understand them. How confident are you in your assessment for each of the three components? What conversations do you need to have with each prospect?

✔ Define the most insightful questions for your buyers, and define what makes strong, weak, and adversarial responses so you are prepared for the answers you might get.

✔ What are the key factors you need to know to determine if a prospect is ready to fully benefit from the solution you offer?

CHAPTER 5
Be An Educator

So far we have laid out the idea that it's better to solve puzzles than to play games, explored the importance of knowing which pieces you carry around, and explained how to find and understand prospects who want to solve puzzles. Now we're ready to sit down on the same side and start solving that puzzle.

But before you can assemble the pieces, you need to put them all on the table. In selling, this step translates to education. By educating your prospects, you help them understand that you are not only unique, but also uniquely qualified to solve the problem they face.

Effective education cannot be taken for granted; in fact, the lack of it is often a point of failure. How many times do promising sales opportunities end with a whimper and a sigh and one of these conclusions?

- "They didn't really understand what we offered."
- "They need us, but they don't realize it."
- "We're so well qualified for this project, but that didn't seem to get through to them."

It's bad enough to lose business because the buyer prefers a different solution. That hurts, but it happens. (Nobody converts every qualified prospect.)

But when prospects decline to buy because they don't understand what you offer or how much you can help them, it's worse than just a lost opportunity. The effort invested feels like a complete waste of time. Sadly, sellers often bring this problem on themselves by failing to educate their prospects. They resist sharing information, they focus on the wrong areas, or they share ineffectively.

The good news is that these are all fixable problems. In this chapter we explain why it is more important than ever to embrace the role of educating your prospects. We will define the areas where you must teach and where to draw boundaries on what you share. We will also discuss how to educate efficiently and effectively through the third-party story.

Why We Don't Always Educate and Why We Must

A Same Side pitch that connects the target customer's problem to your solution is a great way to start the conversation. In most cases, however, buyers will not reach for a credit card without learning more—nor should they. At that point, your most important function is to educate.

All successful educators must be confident in the subjects they teach. How you approach your role as an educator will reveal the answers to three critical questions:

- Is your value proposition compelling enough?
- Are you committed to educating your customers?
- Can you convey your message effectively?

These questions are interdependent. If you don't have confidence in your value proposition—if you're not *certain* that there are puzzle-builders out there who desperately need your pieces to make their pictures look right—then you will feel less committed to the idea of sharing it. So before you try to educate prospects about something you feel mediocre about, revisit your value proposition. If you are not highly enthusiastic about how you have defined your role in the marketplace, then you might want to reread Chapter 2, Be Unique.

When you can define your role clearly, share dramatic success stories, and differentiate yourself from others, teaching will be far easier. Even so, you might still be unclear about how much to share. That is natural, especially given the legacy of the game mentality in selling.

If you have doubts about whether (or how much) you should educate your prospects, that uncertainty will be conveyed and the prospect will be confused or unimpressed. So let's address the reasons you might resist the role of an educator.

The Fear of Sharing Too Much

Withholding information is standard when you are playing games. The best poker players never reveal what their cards are. They hold them "close to the vest." Sometimes, even after a hand is finished, a losing player may still keep his cards hidden so as to not reveal his strategy.

Protective tactics like these make sense in the adversarial trap. After all, someone is going to win and someone is going to lose. Bluffing is part of the game. Has this type of thinking infected your sales team? It might sound like one of these statements:

> "Why do they need to know that now? We'll tell them after they pay us."

> "Let's leave it vague, so we'll have some options once we learn more about their situation."

> "If we reveal our process, they might just do it themselves."

> "If they see the full cost of implementation up front, they'll run away."

These statements represent legitimate questions and concerns that may reflect getting burned in the past. Maybe a one-time prospect copied original concepts from your proposal and shared them with your competitor. Or a potential anchor client pushed hard for price concessions and then stayed with their incumbent vendor—they were simply using you to negotiate with their existing vendor. Perhaps a would-be buyer engaged you for several sessions of design that turned out to be free consulting.

When negative experiences drive the approach to selling, the seller is often doomed to stay in the adversarial trap. Has your team made a vow of "we'll never let that happen again" related to sharing information with a prospect? If so, you may first want to weigh whether that defensive posture has cut short other opportunities. Second, keep reading the guidelines in this chapter to see if anything we suggest is likely to lead to those negative outcomes. When done correctly, education should not open your company to being taken advantage of.

The Reluctance to Be Pushy

Other sellers might resist educating their prospects for an entirely different reason: because it seems like a "hard sell." They prefer a style that is not aggressive or in any way pushy, and fear that guiding a prospect through too much information might damage the relationship.

It is important to note here the distinction between educating and convincing. Some traditional techniques of objection handling may feel more like convincing, or like showing prospects enough data so they realize that their concerns about a purchase are wrong.

The goal of being an educator is not to convince, but to include a prospect in your perspective or knowledge base so that you build a common, mutual understanding. If you are truly Finding Impact Together, there will be some areas where the client needs your perspective and expertise to see the impact.

Why You Have to Be an Educator

Being an educator will confirm the fit, increase your likelihood of sales, and set you up for greater success and impact when you do sell. If those benefits aren't enough of an incentive, here's one more reason to be an educator: you have to.

Information Is Available and Expected

A generation ago, sellers could get by and even thrive by hiding or controlling information. Today that approach will not succeed because of three emerging realities.

REALITY 1: The age of asymmetrical information is over.

Businesses used to depend on having access to information that others didn't have. For example, repair technicians for home appliances once had exclusive access to parts and schematics that are now a few clicks away. Similarly, thirty years ago, auto dealers kept factory invoices for cars locked in a safe, so that not even the salespeople knew the costs basis. Now you can find retail and wholesale costs for virtually any car, and multiple dealerships, in just seconds.

Any value proposition that depends on asymmetrical information is quickly evaporating. If one of your competitors has not yet posted a white paper that describes your company's expertise and operations to 80 percent accuracy or better, it is probably coming soon.

That leads us to the next reason to be an educator.

REALITY 2: Your secrets are probably not really secrets.

There are more than seven million patents registered in the USPTO. Many of those filers hoped to become millionaires, and a few of them did. But it is rare that ideas in themselves are extremely valuable; the lion's share of the work and the reward come with applying those ideas.

In your business, consider the possibility that your trade secrets and intellectual property might not be the treasure you hoped they would be. As with the fabled McDonald's Big Mac, your special sauce might just be salad dressing.

> **Buyer's Perspective:** *When sellers come in and start talking about all of their proprietary knowledge and technology, I get uncomfortable. My gut tells me that most of the information is smoke and mirrors. Plus, I know that the more proprietary it is, the more expensive it will be.*

REALITY 3: Your toughest competitors are two search words away.

The next time you have a free minute, go online and pull up your favorite search engine. Type the words "competitors to" and then the letter "a," and watch the auto-complete window below your text input box. Do you see the names of some companies you recognize, and some you don't? Next, change the "a" to "b," and take another look at the auto-fill options. Interesting?

Now instead of "a" or "b," type "competitors to" and—are you sitting down?—your own company name (or your category, if you are a smaller business). The Internet, search engines, and easy access to competition are not likely to go away.

Teachers Are Needed and Valued

The ubiquity of information might suggest that the role of the educator is less important. In fact, the opposite is true: because there is so much information, there is a desperate need for teachers who can navigate the sea of data. Buyers need to find the right information in the right context.

These new realities do not imply that you should not have any secrets, should never charge for information, and must answer every last question a prospect asks. Being an educator does not mean that you must or should offer full transparency into your practices, technology, and economics.

The key takeaway is that getting access to competition and information is easier than ever before. Information can be found quickly and alternate vendors can be readily identified, making it even more important to get on the same side as the buyer, and stay there. You can do that by being an effective educator who teaches buyers what they need to know.

Education That Is Buyer-Focused, Not Product-Focused

For many people, education in the sales process means product education. The traditional thinking is that prospects need to know all about the product or service—what features it has, how it works, and how it differs from the competition's.

Product-driven education may not be completely wrong, but it is misleading. Educating is not about the product or even about the seller; it's about the buyer. Education begins with the buyer and ends with the buyer. More specifically, it begins with the buyer's challenge and ends with the buyer's overcoming the challenge. Everything you need to teach connects to that beginning and that end.

Throughout the process, keep thinking FIT: the buyer and seller are Finding Impact Together. Education as a part of selling is not academic or theoretical. You are teaching with a goal of action. Your tactics need to reflect this goal.

103

It's worth repeating: the education you provide to your prospects should begin with their challenge and end with their overcoming that challenge—not incidentally, with your help along the way.

Challenge ... solution ... success! These are the components of a great story. In fact, a great story is the best way to educate.

Mastering the Third-Party Story

Although brochures, white papers, and statistics can be useful tools, they are best suited to building agreement on facts. In the quest for action, the student (or buyer) needs to actively gain insights and come to realizations.

Our favorite tactic in helping a prospect move to action is the third-party story. The third-party story shares a challenge or success to which a listener can relate. It offers an opportunity for a buyer to buy in and say, "Yes, that's just like me!"

Third-Party Stories Illuminate the Problem

Here are a few examples of third-party stories used to illustrate the impact of a prospect's challenge:

> "Some of our customers find that after the training, their team doesn't really have the tools to follow up. How might that be a challenge for your organization?"

> "Several of my clients have excellent CFOs who keep an eye on cost, but find that from week to week they are dealing with more strategic issues, like company financing and investor relationships, so they could use some help getting their savings projects off the ground. How common is that?"

"Some companies find that while the local print shop has good prices, they end up spending too many hours on design and communication. How do you address that?"

"A client in your sector was talking to me recently about the challenges they face in finding qualified technical personnel. What is your secret to avoiding that challenge?"

The components are simple: a real example with a problem that the listener might relate to, and then an invitation with an open-ended question. This approach marks an important distinction from the medical analogy: the goal is not for you to provide a definitive diagnosis, but for you and the client to reach a conclusion together. As you aim to uncover the truth efficiently, recognize that what seems critical or obvious to you might not be important to the person in front of you.

Third-Party Stories of Success

Using a third-party story to educate buyers about the impact of their problem will help them acknowledge and understand the costs of their current situation. It is equally important to paint a vivid "after" picture of success.

Again, a third-party story is extremely effective and is the best way to promote your qualifications while you give the buyer a taste of the good future that awaits. Since the story is about someone else, it allows the listener to evaluate without feeling defensive. A key benefit of the third-party story is that it is not about the person in front of you at that time. Rather, it is a safe reference to someone else.

One note here: a third-party story is often more effective without a specific name, so you can present it that way. In any case, before you do share names of companies or individuals, be sure to get approval in writing.

When Ian speaks with companies about the Entice, Disarm, and Discover process, he could tell them that they should implement it in their business. But a third-party story is more compelling:

> One of my client organizations was calling companies for whom they knew they could have a huge impact, but their message was falling on deaf ears. They were seeing a 1 percent response rate. For every hundred calls they made, they got one meeting. Not only was it frustrating, but they also didn't realize how much the effort was costing them.
>
> They went through a process to define the problems they solve, and now they call using the Entice, Disarm, Discover approach. How do you think their results have changed? They now get a 30 percent response rate. How do you think that approach might affect your type of business?

The third-party story provides a comfortable way to let someone relate to a situation as if he is viewing it from the outside. From this position, the listener can think, "I'd like to have a story like that."

Educating on the Impact of Your Solution

The third-party story above illustrates the impact that Ian's solution had on a client. Just as the buyer is more important than the product, *the impact of your solution is much more important than the solution itself.* Buyers need to understand that you are uniquely qualified to solve their problem, but those qualifications usually don't come from what you sell or how you deliver. Buyers are most interested in knowing that you understand the problem completely and that you can guide them to a resolution with results.

We're not saying that the product or service doesn't matter—of course it matters. But in the conversation about impact, the particulars of your solution and experience have relevance only as they directly relate to either the buyer's challenge or your solution to it.

In fact, providing too much information about your qualifications and product features presents not just one but two paths to the adversarial trap. First, sellers are more likely to be concerned about disclosing too much sensitive information or to feel like they need to prove themselves. Second, buyers who are presented with too many details can feel like they're being dazzled and sold to.

Making the solution itself more important than the solution's impact for the buyer caused a huge loss for a company selling to one of Jack's clients, as described in the following story.

> Ed and George were presenting to a national non-profit about a training program that would be worth seven figures over three years. The two men had built a highly successful company with many recognizable brand names as clients, and their company had become one of two finalists vying for the job.
>
> They flew across the country for the meeting. Ed began with a quick thank-you and then launched into

some background about the training company. Then he shared MORE background about the company. Five minutes in, the non-profit executives were exchanging glances and rolling their eyes. Ed continued. He seemed to be speaking more quickly than usual, and he detailed the high-profile clients the company had won, the projects they had taken on, and the truly impressive results that ensued.

Finally, after twelve minutes that seemed like forty-five, Ed finished his introduction and said, "so now let's talk about your goals."

Though a good conversation followed and the company was highly qualified, the executives were lost. Their comments after the meeting suggested that the long biographical preamble did more to hurt the sellers than to help them:

"Those other companies they work with are pretty different from us."

"I think they'd just put us into the same category; I'm not sure they really understand our particular needs."

"Do you think we'd be as important as their other customers that are national names?"

Ed and George suffered from an extremely common premise in sales. They started with their qualifications, instead of with the buyer's problem.

In the context of our puzzle metaphor, this is like finding someone who says he wants to work on a puzzle, and then telling him all about your pieces in great depth before you realize that he's working on a crossword puzzle and you have a cardboard jigsaw puzzle.

Educating Is Another Round of Qualifying

Buyers will sometimes drill down on specific parts of the solution that the sellers are excited to talk about. So you may be asking yourself: are Ian and Jack suggesting that educating buyers about your outstanding qualifications or industry-leading technology in response to their questions is a bad thing?

The central concept is that any diversion from the buyer's challenge decreases your chances of having an impact. This is true even when the buyer leads the diversion. (We'll discuss this more in Chapter 6, Focus on the Fit.)

Educating the prospect is another step in qualifying the opportunity, for both the buyer and the seller. To confirm that your puzzle pieces fit together in a way that can deliver high impact, the buyer's organization needs to:

1. Have the problem or challenge that you can help them address
2. Be in the right demographic categories
3. Be willing to spend money to solve the problem
4. *Believe that YOU can help them*

As you read the last item, we want to note that at this point in the sales cycle, it may seem that the prospect is qualifying you as the seller. But there are only faint lines between being qualified, being evaluated, being judged, and being rejected. When those lines blur, there is a high danger of winding up in the adversarial trap, ending the cooperative, Same Side spirit you worked so hard to build.

Our assertion is that as you continue Finding Impact Together, it is better to see even the education process as another layer of qualifying the opportunity. Part of the buyer's qualification is his belief that you can help his organization. But we'll say it again: that belief will be based on your understanding of the buyer's situation, much more than on your experience, product, and features.

Turning Questions About the Seller into Questions About Impact

When the buyer grills you with questions, it may seem like you have to provide answers, but the best response is often another question in return. Here are a few examples of common buyer questions and ways you can artfully redirect them to a conversation about the buyer's challenge and your solutions.

The fact is that if you answer immediately, there is a good chance that you won't yet have enough information to answer properly. It is in neither your interest nor the client's to answer a question before you understand the underlying reason for it. Consider the following three examples:

Buyer's question: Exactly how long will it take for you to fix this problem?

Seller's response question: That is a common question. At this point I'm not sure if we know enough to give an accurate answer. Once we learn more about the problem, if we can fix it, we can let you know how long it would take. How long have you been dealing with this challenge?

> **Buyer's question:** "Have you served other companies in our sector?"
>
> **Seller's response question:** *"Even though we have served others in your sector, those examples may or may*

not be relevant, depending on your situation. We may have clients in other sectors where the situation is an exact match with your situation. I don't yet know enough about your situation to know which example is most appropriate to share. Can you tell me more about how this problem is affecting your company?"

Buyer's question: "Do you use technology X like your competitor does?"

Seller's response question: "*Technology X is good technology. What is it about that technology that you think would be helpful to address your company's challenge?"*

It may feel unnatural to respond to a buyer's question with a different question instead of just answering. There's a good chance that responding in this manner contradicts the way you have been trained and the way you have sold. Even though you know that everything needs to relate to the prospect's challenge, it may take some practice to gracefully guide the conversation away from details and toward impact. (In his seminars, Ian includes an experiential learning exercise in which attendees pair up and ask each other questions, then practice responding to those questions with more questions instead of answers. After some awkwardness and laughter, participants learn to turn the spotlight back to the questioner.)

It's About You, But It's Really Not About You

The shift from product-based education to buyer-based education may seem subtle, but it is profound. It can change the tone of the conversation from a defensive grilling to a cooperative exploration. By definition, it changes the focus of the conversation from the buyer to the seller.

This is not a matter of charity or humility. This shift is necessary because the path to you goes through the buyer.

There's an old comical line attributed to an over-talkative, self-centered person after minutes of spouting off:

> "... but enough about me. Let's talk about you—what do you think of me?"

The guiding principle on educating your customer is just the opposite. It's as if you were saying:

> "Enough about you and your problem. Let's talk about me—how might I fit in to solving your problem?"

If you are selling, then it's about you. When you are *solving*, not *selling*, the path back to you goes through the buyers.

Putting Boundaries Around Education

We have stressed the importance of connecting all customer education to the prospects' challenges. The most important subjects in that education are the impact of the buyer's problem and the impact of your solution. Other relevant subjects are industry trends, your product's features, and the competitive strengths of your solution versus others.

Of course, the buyer may ask for information that is not related to the fit. How much education is too much, and how do you respond to questions that you don't want to answer?

The first key to avoiding the adversarial trap is to not be offended. Remember the adage that you never know what you can get unless you ask. Many of us have been trained to expect free information, and your competitors may be training your prospects to expect the same.

> **Buyer's Perspective:** *Vendors sometimes seem offended when we ask a lot of questions. Our job is to learn as much as we can, as inexpensively as possible, and then make the decision that is best for our company.*
>
> *It is fully ethical to ask companies to provide information and even consulting, as long as you are up front about the context in which you ask. It is also fully acceptable for a company to say "no," and a refusal does not necessarily end the conversation.*

Another thing to remember is that the individual asking the questions might not be the end-user of your services. This is especially true when companies use a Request for Proposal (RFP). If the guy managing a procurement seems like a jerk ... well, he might be. But the company might still be filled with mostly wonderful people.

Education vs. Free Consulting

When we talk about the importance of education, this does not mean that we encourage you to provide free consulting. The main difference is that education informs your potential client about industry trends or similar challenges faced by other clients and the way you helped them solve those challenges. Free consulting, on the other hand, occurs when you describe the specific solution for a client. Once you set these parameters, it will be easier to determine whether you are educating or giving away free consulting.

We recommend setting guidelines establishing what you will give away and what you will not, and holding firm to those policies. Here are two basic guidelines:

- Give away general information.
- Don't give away the specific, customized application of information.

And here are a few examples:

A software company could share a report on best design practices, but would not draft a specific design for the prospect until the sale is made.

An outsourcing company would share their general implementation plan, but not meet with the team and begin discussions until the buyer has committed.

A marketing company might share a white paper on effective content marketing, but would not design a specific campaign for a prospect.

As information is applied to the specific context of an individual company or situation, it begins to cross the line from information to consulting. Depending on your field, the expectations may vary, but it is up to you to decide how much to share. When a buyer asks for what you consider to be free consulting, you need to consider the likelihood of that buyer's becoming a great long-term customer.

The Right Perspective on Free Consulting

Just because your competition is providing free consulting, that does not mean you should follow their lead. In most cases, customers respect companies that offer education but also make it clear how far they can go without a fee.

If you were a high-end restaurant, would you be threatened by the food court vendor giving away free samples? The food court vendor might be competing with other food court stands, but none of them are truly your competitors. Educating your customers about the care you take in sourcing and preparing your products might help them appreciate your value. You could even share a story about a company that won a huge contract after entertaining customers in your restaurant.

Which kind of customer are you seeking? There are people and companies that are constantly looking to get things for free or for the lowest price possible. If you are offering something of value, focus on those who are willing to pay for it.

Put Same Side Selling to Work

You can get on the Same Side by educating your prospects. Being an educator is more needed than ever, but traditional product-based training is often ineffective and sometimes distracting. Buyers and their challenges must be at the core of education. Third-party stories allow your prospects to gain their own insights and are more likely to inspire action. Set boundaries so that when prospects ask for too much information, you can politely lead the discussion back to something productive for both of you.

- ✔ On a scale of 1–10, how confident are you in your value proposition? If you are not 100 percent confident, then you need to adjust your message.
- ✔ Have you been burned from sharing too much information in the past? What was that experience like? How would you approach that differently?

- ✔ What third-party stories will help your prospects better understand the problem that you solve? Write down two or three stories, and practice sharing them in your next sales meeting.
- ✔ What third-party stories will help your prospects better understand your solution and success? Write down at least three.
- ✔ What are the two most common qualifying questions that you face? What responses could you use for each one to qualify the impact of the prospect's problem and your solution?

CHAPTER 6
Focus on the Fit

Imagine that you are sitting at the table looking at puzzle pieces. You think you see a match. As you pick up one piece and start to position it near another that looks like a fit, your partner at the table protests:

> "Not so fast—let's not put those pieces together quite yet. First I have a few questions: Where did you get that piece? How much did it cost? What's it made of?"

Can you feel your chair moving from the same side to the opposite side as the puzzle turns into a game? Perhaps you've had a similar feeling in the sales process, when the buyer asked a question like one of these:

> *"What is the procedure you use to do that? We need to understand your methods better."*

> *"Your competitor is using technology X on their back-end. Is that what you use?"*

> *"Do you have certification in XYZ?"*

We have proposed that the how and what in your solution are far less important than understanding the buyer's problem and your solution to it. Yet the how and what are almost always part of the conversation. It's natural for buyers to ask questions like the ones above, and for sellers to want to share details of their solutions.

The problem arises when the details take center stage, and either the seller or the buyer loses sight of the overall impact. This distraction can sidetrack progress toward building value, and it can easily pull both sides into the adversarial trap.

In this chapter we explain how to keep your sales conversation focused on results instead of resources, and how to establish clear boundaries of expertise that will serve you throughout the relationship. Keeping the focus on the fit will help you stay on the same side and deliver impact.

Never Lose Sight of the Buyer

It won't surprise readers at this point that the buyer must remain at the center of the conversation. Everything should tie back to the buyer, the buyer's problem, or the solution. Maintaining this focus requires that we revisit some widely accepted selling wisdom.

Go Beyond Features and Benefits

In the early days of mass advertising, marketers defined a distinction between features and benefits:

> A feature is an attribute of a product or service—some way to describe it.

> A benefit is the ultimate good that comes to the buyer.

Features lead to benefits. The conventional wisdom is that good marketing and advertising emphasize the benefits, and that is why people buy. As a classic example, people don't buy Volvos because they have more airbags than other cars; people buy Volvos because they are perceived as being safe.

The advice to focus on benefits rather than features is helpful in Same Side Selling. (It's also insufficient, as we will see in the coming paragraphs. But we'll take one step at a time.) After all, it is the benefit that is more closely connected to solving the client's problem. A posture of solving, not selling, naturally builds off of the benefit. When a seller-buyer conversation centers on features, it is far more likely to have a tone of selling.

Sometimes a buyer drives this tone, and sometimes the seller creates it.

The Temptation to Promote Features

At the beginning of this chapter, we shared some common phrases that buyers use to zero in on features. But this feature-centric thinking doesn't just come from the buyer. Many sellers draw attention to features:

> "Our system represents over six million dollars invested over three years. There's nothing else like it in the marketplace."

> "We have the largest database of _____ in the state."

> "We have been in business longer than any of our competitors."

> "Our people are all certified in XYZ."

We hear these types of claims on a daily basis, and it may seem important to present our qualifications when we are selling. But if the buyer perceives these statements to be boasts or exaggerations, this perception may move the buyer closer to the adversarial trap.

More important, claims like these are rarely related to the buyer's problem. If I am facing litigation related to a zoning matter in Florida, is it important to me that the law firm I am considering is a full-service firm with offices in twelve cities across the country? Details that are not related to the buyer are distractions.

It can take extreme discipline for a CEO to practice self-restraint in effusing about her team's achievements, but that enthusiasm must be contained and pointed directly at the specific problem the buyer is talking to her about. If it isn't, it dilutes the attention of the buyer in the best case. (Think back to the "hundred pennies" analogy in Chapter 2.) The worst case is that it can send a message to the buyer that the seller is too busy congratulating himself to listen well. (This situation is illustrated in the story of Ed and George in Chapter 5.)

When the Buyer Fixates on Features

Sometimes the buyer can drive the emphasis on features. Perhaps buyers saw a demo they loved, they got to know a consultant they trust, or they heard from a colleague at a different company about a technology that will solve their problems.

> **Buyer's Perspective:** *There are times when someone in the executive team fixates on one feature or product attribute and sees it as the cure-all. I call it the "CEO crush," and it can hurt the buying process if it's too much of a factor. For one thing, it kills any bargaining power, but more important, it might not really be the best solution to the problem at hand.*

The "CEO crush" presents an interesting challenge for the seller. In fact, it may even look like a moral dilemma. For example, if potential buyers are so crazy about our technology that they're eager to sign the contract right now, should we slow them down and make sure they are more focused on their problems and the results? Why not just make them happy and give them what they are enthusiastically ready to buy?

Consider this: When potential clients come to you suggesting that they already know which of your products or features they need, which is more common: a) they end up needing exactly what they originally suggested; or b) they end up needing something that is a little different from what they originally suggested? Ian has asked this question of nearly a thousand CEOs and executives. The universal answer is that it is more common that clients end up needing something a bit different from what they thought they needed when they self-diagnosed. So, if we just reply to their requests, we might be selling them the wrong thing—even though they asked for it.

Get Back to the Buyer's Challenge

Forgive the repetition, but a seller's features are NEVER as important as the buyer's problem. In fact, they are relevant only as they address the problem. Discussing features apart from how they directly apply to the client's situation is a waste of energy.

It is not about you. It is not even about your achievements or capability. It is about the client's problem. Clients don't want your brilliance and gadgets; they want results.

Results Are What Really Matter

Let's define an important term that is more important than the feature and even surpasses the feature's benefit: the *result*. The result adds purpose to the benefit. You can think of a result as the benefit specific to the client. If you take the time to educate clients and get to the truth about their needs, you will know each client's desired result.

Imagine that you are in the business of providing recruiting services to consulting companies. You meet a prospect and identify her organization's problem: they have not been able to hire enough qualified people to staff a large contract they recently won, which means they are losing revenue. You are able to offer them not just a general benefit of making qualified hires, but the specific result of greater revenue at their company. Will they pay for that?

(The answer is YES!)

The term "results" is necessary because "feature" is about the product, and "benefit" is based on the feature. Neither term originates with the buyer or her problem. That's fine if you are just selling or playing a game of sales. To sell from the same side, though, you need to come from the buyer's point of view. The best way to accomplish this is for you and the buyer to focus on the results.

Sell Results Instead of Resources

To learn more about why results surpass even the fabled benefit, let's turn our attention to one of the most common and subtle adversarial traps: a focus on resources instead of results.

Is the Buyer Looking for a Tool or Something More?

A resource is essentially a tool. It is a means to an end. In people terms, adding resources means making a hire. The hire could be virtual—vendor support or extended staff on another team. When a person buys a tool, it's up to the buyer to use it correctly and to get the right results. You wouldn't return a hammer to a hardware store and say, "Something's wrong with this hammer—the deck I built looks terrible!"

In contrast, a results purchase solves a problem. Buying results is more comprehensive. It implies that *the risk shifts to the seller*, because the seller will manage the resources to make sure the job gets done. The buyer is paying money to remove a problem. The buyer is buying the *expectation of an outcome, not the supply of a resource.*

In some ways, the discussion of resources versus results parallels the idea of features versus benefits. But it is misleading to suggest that resources are what you buy and results are why you buy. That conception implies that all sellers sell resources, and that there's no meaningful difference between selling resources and selling results. In fact, the difference is far more than semantic.

A Results-Based Purchase Means a Different Mindset

In some cases, the difference between a resource-based purchase and a results-based purchase shows up in the contract and on invoices. In a customer service outsourcing agreement, fees could be based on the number of hours worked (resource-based) or on the number of trouble tickets successfully brought to resolution (results-based). Of course, these different arrangements can have many implications in terms of business and legal risks.

But even when the difference between selling resources and selling results is not literal or contractual, the mindset is extremely important. When buyers believe they are buying resources rather than results, they focus on the specifications of the resource, rather than on the likelihood of reaching the desired outcome.

Examples of Selling Resources versus Selling Results

What does this distinction look like? Let's look at a few examples of businesses we understand, and discuss the difference between selling resources and selling results.

> A resource-based lawn services company sells hours of labor for such tasks as mowing yards and weeding flower beds.

A results-based lawn services company sells well-groomed yards that its clients can enjoy on the weekends.

A resource-based accounting firm sells on-call accounting support, report preparation, and strategic input.

A results-based accounting firm sells compliance, reliable reporting, and peace of mind.

A resource-based customer relationship management (CRM) software company sells a software package that includes service modules and database management.

A results-based CRM software company sells effective customer management and communication.

On the surface, the items in each pair look similar. They might be nearly identical in price and delivery. Yet the distinction between selling resources and selling results is profound in the way the purchase is viewed by the seller and the buyer. It shapes the perception and reality of the sales process and the ongoing relationship.

Selling Results Even When Billing for Resources

A common view is that professional services are always resourced-based transactions. But even traditional law firms can sell results instead of resources, as we will illustrate here.

Let's say you are facing a legal issue. A client refuses to pay after you clearly delivered exactly what was agreed to in the contract. The client owes you $200,000. You speak with two law firms.

Firm A tells you, "This is exactly the kind of thing that we handle. Here is a list of our hourly rates. We'll need a $5,000 retainer to get started. Just sign our agreement, and we can send them a letter right away."

Firm B, on the other hand, says, "It must be frustrating when you have delivered as promised and they are not paying their bills. There are three possible scenarios that I want you to know about so there are no surprises. In some cases, just knowing that a law firm is involved will motivate them to send you the money or ask for a settlement. In that case, getting you paid might cost about $2,500. If they are a bit more confrontational, then it could take longer, and we typically see a resolution with an investment of about $25,000. If it ends up going to court, a matter like this could cost $70,000 to get resolved. How would you like to proceed?"

Can you see that Firm A is selling resources (hours of labor) and Firm B is selling results (reaching a resolution)? Whatever your field, you can sell results instead of resources. Selling results will help you Focus on the Fit and not be distracted by the small stuff.

Being Unique Allows You to Sell Results

At this point, there may still be a voice in your head wondering if you are a resource seller or a results seller. That's OK; let's take a minute and tie this back to differentiation.

In Chapter 2, Be Unique, we explained how critical it is to know the specific value that you bring to the marketplace. It means, to borrow Zig Ziglar's terminology, that you are a "meaningful specific" rather than a "wandering generality." You have defined a unique offering, a place that you call your territory. You own your own hill, rather than sharing someone else's mountain.

Armed with the knowledge of how your pieces are shaped differently than others, you are prepared to position yourself as a seller of *results*. Selling results doesn't mean you have to take more risks and guarantee results, though in some cases you might. It means that you have:

- A track record of relevant success
- Confidence and expertise

When you sell results, you are claiming specific expertise to solve a problem better than the buyer's organization can solve it on their own. This is an essential premise of your sale, and it must be clear to you as the seller and to the buyer.

The Need for Clear Boundaries of Expertise

The results-based sale carries an important implication: the seller is the expert on delivering the results. To maintain focus on the fit, both the seller and the buyer must be confident in the boundaries of their mutual expertise.

This principle is intuitive for many familiar purchases: if I need an appendectomy or an addition to my house, I know that whomever I buy from (the surgeon, the contractor) must have the appropriate knowledge and skill. I don't expect them to ask me, "so, what kind of incision would you like?" or "does this look level to you?" We know that they are the experts.

How Murky Expertise Leads to Micromanaging

For many services, the boundaries of expertise are less obvious, and that murkiness can cause problems. *Ambiguous expertise* is a foundational flaw that causes many buyer-seller conversations to devolve back to a game-based mentality. When it is unclear who the expert is, producing maximum value between the buyer and seller becomes much harder. Instead of focusing on how the pieces fit together, the conversation can sink deep into the weeds, often spurred by a sentence like one of the following:

> "How do you handle configuration management? Our IT group has specific standards."

> "Will we get to approve anyone you hire?"

> "We need these custom reports to monitor at the level of detail we're used to."

Does this sound like Finding Impact Together, or more like an elementary school teacher checking your work? When you feel over-managed as a seller, you may need to assess whether you are selling results or resources and whether you have effectively established your expertise.

Buyer's Perspective: *We're looking for partners that have experience and a confident point of view about their solution. We want them to know the details, and that's why we pay them. If we have to worry about how they're doing their job, it's worth much less to us—we might as well just hire extra staff.*

Define Your Expertise

The first step in establishing your expertise is being able to articulate it. (Revisit Chapter 2, Be Unique, if needed.) Assuming that you are confident in your unique selling proposition, you may benefit from a "who's the expert?" conversation with your client. It's worth using a whiteboard or a piece of paper to write down a simple two-column list. One column is for your areas of expertise, and the second represents the buyer's expertise. To illustrate with a website design company, it might look something like this:

Seller's Expertise	Buyer's Expertise
Website optimization	Buyer's company
Technical objectives	Business goals
Search engine optimization (SEO)	Website content
Technical application	Website look and feel

Table 6-1: Separate Areas of Expertise

As simple as this exercise appears, it is likely to generate useful questions. In the example above, is it obvious that the buyer would be the expert in the website's look and feel? You can imagine that a seller might assume that, or might assume the opposite. The expertise list erases assumptions and provides clarity.

If your team is getting stuck on defining where the expertise lies, it may help to start from a different point that identifies where expertise is shared.

Address Shared Expertise

Jack recently helped a company review its relationships with communications vendors, which had become problematic. Company management believed that they were spending too much money in this area and their efforts seemed disorganized Early in the process, the team tried to answer the question,

"Who is the expert?" It proved difficult to cleanly separate where expertise resided, so we added a third column for shared expertise and completed the table to reflect the current reality. Jack calls this table an "expertise map," and it looked like the following example:

Seller's Expertise	Shared Expertise	Buyer's Expertise
Marketing tactics	Marketing strategy	Buyer's company
	Online strategy	Buyer's overall strategy
Advertising placement	Customer knowledge	Customers

Table 6-2: The Expertise Map Reveals Overlapping
Areas of Expertise

When the team stood back from the whiteboard, they had a collective "a-ha" moment. Every problem they saw in the relationship tied back to shared expertise—that is, areas where it was unclear who the expert was.

"No wonder we're arguing about what the customer wants—we both think we're the experts in that."

"We're paying for them to create our marketing strategy, but we have our own people who do that."

"Online has been so hard because we keep stepping on each other's toes!"

"Shared expertise" is a nice way to say that expertise ownership is unclear. This uncertainty can create many problems as a client relationship develops. If the buyer bases a purchase decision on the wrong understanding of who the expert is, that confusion has the potential to ruin the relationship and erase any impact that you may have created.

When Expertise Is a Sensitive Subject

Part of your job as the seller is to ensure that buyers have a clear understanding of your expertise. When they trust your expertise over their own in an area, they will trust you on the details and it will be easier to focus on the fit.

Getting to that understanding can be delicate when the expertise you bring encroaches on the buyer's perceived expertise. In some cases it may provoke disagreement on the buyer's team and objections to the sale.

> *"Why should we bring in your company to help with this, when we have a whole group doing this?"*
>
> *"Any changes in _____ have to go through Bill—that's his area."*

Is it worth stirring up these potential objections? What will happen, for example, when the IT manager who is a self-styled social media expert sees in writing that his company is hiring an outside firm to help with social media?

When areas of expertise overlap, it is especially critical to address the boundaries and define them. The sooner the conflict appears and is addressed, the better. You can often resolve the conflict by stepping back and asking questions that bring the focus back to the fit.

Artfully Direct the Client Back to the Fit

When questions or comments reveal that the buyer and seller may have different ideas of how the expertise is divided, it's critical to move the focus back to the fit. Statements and questions like the following can help:

> "We may have gotten ahead of ourselves, so I just want to confirm. Are you looking for help in this area, or do you have it pretty well figured out?"

> "We've had great success with helping many companies about your size achieve lasting results. The recipe that works is one where we can bring all that we've learned and apply our methods. We don't want to do it halfway."

> "How and when will you ultimately measure success on this? If we're agreed on that, are we free to use our tactics as long as we can measure and report on the success?"

We want to stress that these are not manipulative tactics to silence a problem personality on the vendor's team. It is important to seek and listen for the truth. That truth may lead to an adjustment of the buyer's expectations or attitudes, or it may lead to a conclusion that your offering is not a good fit.

Buyers may want to hear a few technical answers to bolster their confidence, and that is fine. But too much emphasis on the how may reveal that the boundary lines of expertise are faint or overlapping. If your prospect will not focus on the fit even after one of these replies, you may need to consider whether his company will be a long-term, high-margin client or is looking for a different type of resource.

If your goal is to have long-term clients and referral business, then it is very much in your interest to make sure your prospect is focused on the fit and the end result. As with getting all of the buyer's puzzle pieces right-side up, maintaining this focus takes discipline—especially when the buyer is ready to buy and is congratulating you on your brilliant product. But your efforts to gently move your prospect's attention from the details to the greater objectives will pay dividends.

Here are some ways to refocus:

"We can't promise that Joe will always be on the project, but if we can define what success looks like and report on that quarterly, we'll make sure that we always get you strong results."

"Our database is a great asset, as you have noted. The real power comes in our ability to use that information to meet your goals. So before we get started, let's make sure we understand those goals."

"Sometimes our clients ask for something specific, and we realize down the road that we failed to ask enough questions, only to discover later that the clients would have been better off with another approach—in many cases, a less expensive approach. Would you mind if we asked a few questions before we get too far down the path?"

Put Same Side Selling to Work

The puzzle pieces you have are your resources. They are relevant, but only because they lead to results. Your pieces are valuable only if they fit the holes in the client's puzzle. If you and the client have trouble seeing why her company needs your products or services, then perhaps your pieces are not a fit for their puzzle.

It is natural for buyers to ask questions about vendor costs, personnel, and process. These factors can all affect the quality and delivery of the end product. But an emphasis on the seller's costs, rather than on the buyer's value, can derail a possibly great deal. Ultimately what matters is the puzzle piece. The people and process behind it matter to the extent that they determine its shape.

Are you looking at each other or looking at the pieces?

✔ Review your biggest client account. Is your arrangement with this client results-based or resources-based?

✔ Think of the most recent conversation you had with a prospect. Estimate what percentage of the time you talked about resources and what percentage you devoted to results.

✔ Review your standard customer agreement. If you had to classify the document as either resource-based or results-based, which would it be? Why?

✔ Of all of your customer relationships, which is farthest from where you would like it to be? For that customer, are the boundaries of expertise clear? If not, create two versions of an expertise map for that relationship: one that reflects the current status, and one that would be the target. Consider reviewing that expertise map with the client.

✔ Create an expertise map for your optimal client engagement.

CHAPTER 7
Don't Force the Fit

Traditional sales training goes deep and wide on how to close the sale, overcome objections, persuade prospects, and upsell buyers. Behind these tactics are two working assumptions: that a sale is better than no sale, and that a bigger sale is better than a smaller sale.

In this chapter we take a different view. We're not arguing that smaller is better or that losing the right deal is a good thing. What we are saying is that *the practice of restraint is more important than upselling*. Being willing to say no—even when the buyer is ready to say yes—is an essential element of Same Side Selling.

Sometimes the fit and impact we seek just aren't there. This reality may be slow to emerge. What looked like a perfect fit from a distance turns out to be something less after getting to the truth. What happens then?

This chapter is about what happens after that disconnect appears. We'll explain what it means for a seller to force the fit instead of showing restraint, and why forcing the fit is so common and so problematic. Then we will explain why restraint can be the best path toward easier selling, more profitable clients, and more referral business. We'll also cover the right way to refer a prospect to someone else so the referral benefits all three parties.

What It Looks Like to Force the Fit

When you force the fit during a sale, you are almost always doing one of the following or a mix of both:

- Selling services outside of your expertise
- Selling a solution to a problem that the client doesn't have or perceive

139

> **Buyer's Perspective:** *Unfortunately, a couple of our vendors are like hammer salesmen. By that I mean they only sell hammers, so to them all of our problems look like nails. This is such a turnoff and it limits the relationship to a very tactical level. It means that instead of getting their help to diagnose our problem, we have to be on guard that they'll try to fix it with the wrong solution. A hammer salesman can never be a trusted advisor.*

The most colorful examples of forcing the fit are blatant and unethical. Think of a dentist over-diagnosing thousands of dollars of unnecessary surgery and repair, or an auto parts store selling the wrong model part for the buyer's car (causing the poor buyer to literally *force the fit*!). No one still reading this book is likely to traffic in such malpractice, and we won't spend time on it here.

But in other cases, forcing the fit is a judgment call. It may even look like wise opportunism. Consider these scenarios:

- A trusted strategy consultant is asked by a CEO to hire a new sales team, and the consultant accepts, even though he hasn't done that type of work before.
- An IT company bids on a job that requires specific technology expertise they do not have in-house. They conclude that they'll figure it out

Are these projects great vehicles for fueling growth and learning for the vendors, while delivering solid value to the clients? Or are they examples of forcing the fit in situations where a better course would be to use restraint?

Later in this chapter, we'll present our framework for double- and triple-checking the fit. First, we'll look at the implicit peril in these opportunities and discuss how a subtle case of forcing the fit can do great harm.

The Hazards of Pushing the Sale

Some readers may still be scratching their heads, wondering why nudging a client closer to a sale can be a bad thing or how closing the deal might be something you *don't want*. If you are thinking that, don't worry—it probably just means that you were paying attention in your previous sales training.

Our puzzle metaphor is useful here. You might pick up two pieces that looked like a fit and move them close to each other. But if they don't match, you're certainly not going to mash them together. Yet in the context of sales, the adversarial trap beckons sellers to make a sale fit, even if it really doesn't.

As an example, let's say that you are selling legal services. You have a client ready to engage your firm on a retainer basis, but you suspect that the client might have only one isolated need. You could certainly provide him with additional legal services under retainer, but he might just need a quick letter and a review of an agreement. Nonetheless, the client is ready to buy.

This is a moment of high drama, at least on the inside. The devil on your shoulder screams "sign the deal!" The angel on your other shoulder whispers "slow down." We'll start by assuming that you listen to the loudest voice and push ahead toward the close. Let's look at what happens next.

Problems Before the Sale

Forcing the fit can kill an opportunity. In our legal services example, if the client realizes before the sale that a full retainer is overkill—*while you are actively closing the sale*—there are several negative outcomes.

- Direct outcome: The prospect won't buy.
- Indirect outcome 1: The client won't trust you, as he might feel somewhat taken advantage of. (Of course, he might just sigh that you were "doing your job," as many people believe it's the job of sales reps to get people to buy things they really don't need. But in that case, he still won't trust you.)
- Indirect outcome 2: The client won't refer you.

This is not only a short-term loss but also a long-term loss.

Problems After the Sale

Another path presents a win—at least in the short term. The client signs the contract and writes the checks. In this case, there are three potential scenarios.

First, everything could work out great: the client might discover additional needs and the retainer might provide value. That's a great outcome: happy seller, happy buyer. (Happy devil, too?) Call it *dumb luck.*

We'll label the second outcome *dumb and happy.* In this case, your instincts proved right—the retainer was not the best option for the client—but he never figured it out. His company muddled along, oblivious to the waste and inefficiency of paying for far more than they needed.

The third outcome we'll call *burned and learned.* (If you prefer the name *sadder but wiser,* that also works.) The buyer figures out, after some period of time, that he is not getting the best value out of your services. He cancels the contract and asks for a refund of the unused retainer, and everyone starts arguing about contract cancellation timelines and fees. (Ugh.)

> **Buyer's Perspective:** *Eighteen months into our engagement with a service provider, we realized we were paying way too much for their services and could do everything at a lower cost with similar results. I'm quite sure we'll never use that vendor again, nor could I refer them to anyone else. It feels like we got taken for a ride.*

It's worth noting that the indirect negative implications discussed earlier are highly likely in the third outcome. The buyer—now a former client—will be less likely to trust you. Even if he gives you the benefit of the doubt and trusts your motive, he won't trust your competence because you did not protect his interests and deliver value. (We don't need to write that he won't refer you—but he won't.)

Why Restraint Is the Best Path

Now let's go back to that point of high drama during the sales process, but assume a different course of action. Instead of forcing the fit and going ahead with the sale, you listen to the angel on your shoulder. You practice restraint by saying "no" (or "not yet") when the buyer is willing to say "yes." Instead, you say, "At this point, my sense is that we could address everything you need in the short term with a simple agreement that will not exceed $3,500. If, along the way, we discover additional areas where you might need our help, we can talk about expanding our agreement at that point. Fair?"

Buyer's Perspective: *Honestly, we sometimes get lazy and commit to a solution or a vendor too soon. If we've been talking to a vendor for weeks, it can be hard to step back and see that committing is not the best path. Taking a step back can look bad internally, but when we rush to buy and implement, it doesn't always serve us well. It can even put our vendors in a tough position. When things don't turn out the way we want, it's always easier to blame the vendor than to admit we made a bad decision.*

Keep in mind that the impetus to force the fit is not always seller-driven. The buyer may be pushing the deal more than you. No matter who's driving the process, though, your caution may be unexpected. When you need to put the brakes on, you can say something like:

> "I hate to slow things down and we do want your business, but let's make sure we're looking at this the right way. We want to move forward with this only if it is the right solution for you. So can we run through the solution and the numbers again?"

What happens next? After further exploration of the value, the client may confirm your instincts and decide it's not the right purchase or not the right time. You lose the sale, but you know you followed your gut in questioning the fit, and the client's conclusion was the same as yours. (You both walk away with your puzzle pieces, looking for the right opportunity to use them.) This is the worst-case scenario for not forcing the fit: perhaps a short-term financial loss, but a sound ethical and long-term decision.

Enhance Your Stature by Being Deliberate

It's also quite possible that when you pause—when you show restraint—the prospect will have a different reaction. At first, you may detect a change in how he sees you. Now you're no longer someone trying to sell retainer-based legal services above all else and acting only in self-interest. With one small step back— one decision not to grasp—you have defined yourself as someone who is carefully mindful of the prospect's best interests.

We want to emphasize that this approach is not charity or weak salesmanship. Nor is it a position of sacrifice or selflessness. It's a matter of seeking the right solution and the right fit. The adversarial trap says that you have to put either yourself first or the buyer first. In Same Side Selling, the buyer and seller aren't looking at each other and sizing up where to slice the pie so everyone gets their share. They are looking at a puzzle and deciding whether they can figure it out together. It's not buyer first or seller first—it's value first.

A homeowner we know was planning a renovation. During a discussion between the homeowner and a construction company, the construction seller said, "It seems like you had good success with another contractor in the past. We focus on people who have had a bad experience with their contractor. Why don't you see what your previous contractor comes up with? If you are not completely satisfied with their proposal, please contact us and we'd be happy to see if we can help."

This seller asked enough questions to discover that the prospect already had a favorite vendor. By doing so, the seller ensured two things: 1) the contractor would not waste time chasing an unlikely win; and 2) if the prospect was not thrilled with the first vendor's proposal, the contractor would have a perfect opportunity to address the concerns when the homeowner would be most receptive to an alternative.

If you ever feel tired of being treated like a salesperson, this may be the key idea you have been waiting for. It's not a new principle, though; consider the words of the ancient historian Thucydides:

"Of all the manifestations of power, restraint impresses men the most."

In a go-getter, competitive world, we have been conditioned to go for it, to make it happen, and to sell ourselves. Forcing the fit is the norm, which makes restraint still more remarkable and more effective.

When the Right Solution Isn't Yours

Van Mensa is one of Nordstrom's all-time most successful salespeople. He also has the dubious distinction of being the person from whom Ian has bought many suits over the years. Shortly before a trip to a cold climate, Ian went to Nordstrom's to shop for a pair of gloves. Van escorted Ian to the men's accessories department, where they began to try the various gloves to see which would be the best fit for Ian's big hands. With none of them fitting well, Ian said, "I'm sure they'll stretch out over time." This was not acceptable to Van.

Van said, "Come with me." They exited the store, and Van escorted Ian to Macy's, at the other end of the mall. They entered the men's accessories department, and Van played the role of personal shopper. He asked the salesperson for a specific brand and size of glove. When Ian put it on, Van asked, "Is that a better fit?" Ian smiled and Van handled the purchase transaction with the Macy's representative. On the walk back to Nordstrom, Van said, "If you have any problems with these gloves, just bring them back to me and I'll take care of it."

Van did more than ensure that Ian found the right pair of gloves; he ensured a lifelong customer. At other times, Ian would start to buy a suit, only for Van to say, "You don't need it. You have a suit just like it in your closet." Ian would go home to find the forgotten suit in his closet. Quite simply, Van would never sell Ian anything he did not need.

Exercising restraint is a powerful long-term strategy to achieve more sales with less effort. This idea may seem contradictory, but no does often lead to *yes*. Just as in the Nordstrom example, finding the right solution for your client (even if it is not your own solution) is what leads to long-term repeat and referral business.

When You Pull Back, They Often Follow

At speaking engagements, Ian teaches restraint with a memorable exercise that gets everyone out of their seats. All attendees pair up, and one person in each pair—the lead—is given instructions which the other person does not see. Then they proceed with a 5-second exercise that is often described as the biggest *a-ha moment* of the day.

Each person stands facing their partner, and then places the palms of their hands against their partners' hands. (This part always generates some giggles, even among mature professionals.) Then, as the partners stand face to face, palm to palm, Ian says "Go," and the lead partners carry out their instructions.

There are two sets of instructions. On the left side of the room, the leads are instructed to push forward with their hands, slowly but firmly. On the right side of the room, the leads are instructed to gently and slowly draw their hands backwards, toward themselves.

Can you guess what happens? It is extremely consistent among the thousands of people who have taken part in the exercise.

The lead "pushers" see the same reaction in more than 95 percent of the situations: they get resistance from their partners, who push back in a contest of strength. In less than 5 percent of the situations, the other people will just quickly pull their hands back.

The lead "pullers" experience one dominant reaction from their partners. Nearly all of them slowly follow the lead person's hands back.

After he passes out hand sanitizer, Ian lands this hands-on learning exercise with two simple messages:

Lesson 1: When you push as a seller, buyers will almost always push back at you or simply pull away altogether. It's a form of the "fight or flight" response. Under pressure, you generally get resistance either with confrontation or with "don't call us, we'll call you."

Lesson 2: If you pull back—if you show restraint—buyers will often follow you where you lead them. At a minimum, you will pique their interest.

When Restraint Leads to the Sale

Is using restraint some sort of manipulative "reverse psychology" trick? It can be, and if you treat it like a gimmick, it probably won't yield long-term results. But if exercising restraint is a genuine action to get on the same side and continue Finding Impact Together, it is likely to be good both for relationships and for sales.

Let's refer to our example of the legal services sale. You, as the seller, have practiced restraint and challenged the fit even though the prospect seemed ready to buy. The client may agree with your instincts and not buy, as we discussed above. But he may be just as likely to follow your hands as you draw them back:

"No, I really think we'll use more of your services, and the retainer is the best solution for us."

"We have some changes coming that will make the retainer even more valuable for us."

"We've been looking for months, and I have approval for this engagement. It's the right move."

Are these the things we want to hear from clients? Absolutely! Not only have they started selling you, but they have also escalated their commitment, thereby increasing their likelihood of success. They have expressed ownership of the buying decision and have better demonstrated their understanding of the benefits. This response does not absolve the seller of ensuring value, but it certainly makes the burden lighter.

There's No Such Thing as a Pushy Ambassador

Sales professionals are not known for restraint; quite the opposite. They're expected to drive toward a sale, whether or not it works well for the customer. Even if you are in the profession of sales, you may have this default perception. Consider the last time you were buying a car, a home appliance, or any other item that required you to talk to a salesperson. Was that salesperson a model of restraint and respect? Or was he just a bit pushy? In short, was he looking to sell or looking to solve?

We've explained and repeated our simple approach of Finding Impact Together and making the client's challenge our main concern. Here's an eloquent description by Seth Godin of the posture we endorse in Same Side Selling:

Your customers need an ambassador. Someone who is open to hearing what they have, need and want, not merely a marketer intent on selling them a particular point of view. Once you understand someone, it's much easier to bring them something that benefits everyone.

And your partners need you to honor the spirit and intent of the deals you do with them. The goal of a long-term relationship isn't to find the loophole that lets you do what you want. (From "Ambassadors and treaties," October 19, 2013, <http://sethgodin.typepad.com/seths_blog/2013/10/ambassadors-and-treaties.html>)

We love the way Seth's concept of being an ambassador conveys the spirit of restraint. An ambassador would never force the fit.

Is It Forcing the Fit or Just Good Selling?

Admittedly, there is no failsafe diagnostic to determine when a seller is forcing the fit. But these questions will point the way:

Question 1: Are you being completely honest and open about the solution?

Honesty is the first standard. If you have in any way misled the buyer, allowed her to have the wrong perception, or overstated your capability, then you are probably forcing the fit.

Question 2: Would your solution be in the best interest of the owners of the buying company?

This question is a bit different from "would the owners *approve* of the purchase?" because it requires you to apply your expertise about your own industry and solution. Think long-term, and try to suspend your healthy bias about your own capability.

Question 3: Would your board agree that this project is in line with your company's strengths and strategy?

There are times when a company sells something outside of the areas in which it has a track record. That doesn't mean it won't work, but the decision should always be aligned with strategy to ensure that the company will be committed to seeing the value through.

If you put the opportunity through these questions, does it look *more* like a fit or less like a fit?

When in Doubt, Bow Out

If the answer is still unclear, the Same Side approach is to err on the side of restraint. This contradicts the Always Be Closing mentality that many (if not nearly all) sales professionals would endorse.

We've analyzed how restraint can clarify the fit, build trust, and position you for future business and referrals. With those benefits, there may be some added risk that you will lose the sale; but then again, it may be a sale that's better to lose. There's also a good chance that as soon as you step away, the buyer will start roping you back in. ("Please let me buy from you!")

This dynamic reflects the potency of restraint. Restraint is both a cause and an effect of Same Side Selling. Practicing restraint doesn't just show that you are not playing a game; it also gets you out of the game.

Sentences That Magically Change Games into Puzzles

Same Side Selling is not a quick fix; it's a mindset, a methodology, and a group of disciplines that require practice to perfect. But if we had to create an instant Same Side treatment, it would be prescribed in the form of restraint. In fact, a few words expressing restraint can serve as a magic spell that instantly brings a conversation out of the adversarial mentality and puts the buyer and seller on the same side. For instance:

"We may not be the best firm to help you with this problem."

"As much as we'd like to work with you, we are not yet sure if we have a great fit."

These admissions echo the Disarm phrases that we covered in Chapter 3, Narrow Your Market, and they have a similar appeal later in the sales process. Buyers do not expect to hear these words from sellers. They find them refreshing and attractive.

> **Buyer's Perspective:** *I've almost never heard a salesperson tell me he couldn't help us. I can think of two specific instances, one of which happened over five years ago. The first thing that struck me was, "For these guys, it's not all about making the sale." The second thing I thought was, "Wow, I'd love to work with them on something."*

Because even the best products, process, and sales talent will miss sometimes, it is important to have a plan for that certain contingency. How do you proceed when you and the buyer have concluded that your pieces don't fit together?

Referring from the Same Side

After the buyer and seller decide together not to force the fit, no one would blame the seller for simply wishing the buyer the best and saying goodbye. They can part as friends and move on in the world. But just because you don't have the pieces the buyer needs, does that mean you can't help solve the puzzle?

Referring another solution or vendor to a potential prospect is a black-belt-level skill in Same Side Selling. It proves beyond any doubt that restraint is not manipulative or some highly disguised form of self-interest. To say "We can't help you with this, but I think I can help you find someone who might be a great fit" erases any lingering adversarial suspicions.

The benefits of referring another solution are well studied and well known, so why do so many sales conversations end with a parting of ways and no referral? Here are a few reasons that salespeople are reluctant to refer another solution:

- They still hope they might get the business, and they don't really want the buyer to hire someone else. (We've worked through these passive-aggressive sentiments already in the chapter. Let's move on.)
- They don't know whom to refer.
- They are afraid that the referred company might not do a good job.
- They fear that the referred company will help not only in this situation, but also in others in which their company is engaged.

We will present several guidelines that will address these concerns and will apply to any referrals to make it more probable that the buyer stays on the same side.

Referral Tip 1: Refer With Full Candor

Referring is an area where full candor is required for self-preservation. When you introduce another potential problem-solver, a misunderstanding or partial truth could hurt *your* reputation. So be proactive and thorough in how you present the referred company.

Share any and all connections. If the company you are referring is a family member or a friend, be sure you say that up front. If you are in a networking group together or you attend the same synagogue or the VP lives in your neighborhood, let the prospect know. By all means, if you have any business affiliation or could benefit from the referral, let the prospect know. Ian often gets asked if he can help with recruiting. Since he does not offer that service, he often refers to a small set of other firms and always says, "I receive absolutely no direct or indirect compensation from them. However, when they find you the right person, it helps us achieve greater success together."

Share your knowledge of the referred company's results. Because you are helping the prospect find a fit, the key word is "results." If you have worked with the referred company multiple times in the past fifteen years and you've seen many of their clients achieve success, then share it! Even if you're not familiar with the referred company's results, the referral can still be helpful—just let the prospect know. The same principle applies if you just found an interesting-looking company on the Internet ten minutes ago.

That brings us to the next principle of referrals.

Referral Tip 2: Research Referrals

Just because you are new in town or have recently changed fields doesn't mean you cannot make helpful referrals. As long as you are candid about your connection, it's fine to refer companies that you don't have firsthand experience with. A good way to do this would be to say:

> "We may not be the best fit right now, but I'd certainly like to help you find a company that can help you. Let me give that some thought and do some research and

get back to you with a few suggestions by the end of the week. Would that be helpful?"

You may be wondering why your Google and Bing efforts would be better than the buyer's. This is an area where an hour of research could be extremely helpful for your former prospect. For one thing, you have different areas of expertise. You know what you're looking for and probably the best terms to search on. You can probably make a call or two to qualify your recommendations. The output doesn't have to be a conclusive marketplace review; simply provide the names of the companies, the websites, and a few reasons that you think they merit further research.

The goal is not to provide an ironclad endorsement, but to help buyers move forward with their search for the right fit. That brings us to the next crucial referral tip.

Referral Tip 3: Refer Multiple Solutions

Referring two companies is much, much better than referring one. (If you know only one, follow the second tip to research and find more possibilities.) Providing multiple referrals for a specific problem helps in several ways. Most important, it relieves you of any perceived ownership of the outcome. You are not promoting the right solution, but simply providing some possible choices. You are encouraging the buyer to continue her search for the right fit.

If you are referring only one vendor, you can simply say to the prospect, "My clients have had great success with them. I'm sure there are other qualified vendors. I'd encourage you to compare two or three vendors before moving forward."

In addition to protecting you as the referrer, submitting multiple solutions has another upside. If you provide introductions or connections to possible vendors, they will appreciate the opportunity even if it doesn't work out for them. Better still, more shots on goal means a greater likelihood that the vendor the buyer chooses will be one that you suggested, so you will still have a role in solving that puzzle.

A Warning: No Favors, No Hookups

In addition to the three "do's" in the principles above, we want to explicitly define an important "don't." Do not refer a buyer to a seller as a *favor to the seller*.

The driving motivation should always be fit. Ideally, you would refer the buyer to other sellers who would practice Same Side Selling and put the FIT first, but their methods are beyond your control. You should certainly do your best to *not* refer someone who will themselves force the fit or who is desperate for business or unclear about their value proposition.

In this case, the analogy of romance and dating is helpful. If you had a friend who was a bit desperate, would you set him or her up with a person you valued, as a favor to your friend? Or would you introduce the two of them, believing that there may be a fit, and leave them to sort it out? This is a meaningful distinction.

By the same token, the referral should not be seen as a "hookup" that absolves the buyer of the need to confirm the fit and the value on his own. If you have a great relationship with a qualified vendor, you might be tempted to put a referral on the fast track by promoting that vendor:

- "These guys would be perfect for you."
- "I've known Jim for years and he will definitely do a great job."

These strong endorsements may seem harmless or even helpful, but they should always be qualified with a dose of restraint:

- "From what I've seen, these guys might be a great fit for this job."
- "I've known Jim for years and he has many satisfied clients; if you guys determine that he's the right fit, I'm sure he will deliver."

The difference again may seem subtle, but it is meaningful. Backing off a little removes any hint of sliminess or the sense of an inside deal. It keeps you on the same side as the buyer.

Can You Refer to a Competitor?

This question relates to Chapter 2, Be Unique. If you have clearly identified your unique value proposition, you should be able to differentiate your company from your perceived competitors. This principle works both ways: it means that you know which types of buyers are better for you, and you know which types are best for your competitors. In fact, the companies are competitors in only a limited sense because your puzzle pieces are unique, and your best prospects will be different from those of your competitors.

In fact, referring a one-time prospect to a perceived competitor is a grand trophy of Same Side Selling. If you have made it there, congratulations.

For more on referrals, we refer you (get it?) to our good friend and referral expert Derek Coburn. In his book, *Networking Is Not Working*, he presents a business development plan based on referring business to others.

Put Same Side Selling to Work

Pushy salesmanship leads directly to the adversarial trap. One of the most effective ways to get on the same side as the buyer (and separate yourself from other salespeople) is to avoid any hint of forcing a solution that may not meet the buyer's requirements. This means being quick to acknowledge that you may not have the right offering, and it may mean even referring the customer to another solution or vendor. Practicing restraint and referral builds your stature with the buyer, and positions you to sell easily and quickly when you do have the right solution.

- ✔ Talk to your sales team about whether your company consistently practices restraint or sometimes forces the fit. Identify specific clients with whom you have forced the fit.
- ✔ Make a list of the competitors you frequently see in the marketplace. Then add some information about which types of clients are the best for each of these firms. Your team can use this information to help confirm that you are the best fit, and as a referral guide for prospects for whom you don't have that ideal fit. (We're not suggesting that you share the list with buyers, but you can use it internally to point them in the right direction.)
- ✔ Count the number of referrals you have made in the last year. If you do not have this information, consider tracking referrals along with your other sales metrics.
- ✔ Identify a sales opportunity that you lost in the last ninety days. If you're not sure of the outcome, write an email that starts, "In case you have not found a great solution yet, I had a few thoughts about whom you might talk to" and then list the companies and your notes about each one.

✔ Conduct a sales meeting in which referrals are the sole agenda item. Share your recent experiences in referring to others and share ideas about how to refer more effectively. (Have your team read this chapter before the meeting.)

CHAPTER 8
Sell Value, Not Price

News flash: Buyers often focus on price. In many cases, your initial conversation with them might be primarily about price. We know that can be frustrating for sellers, but remember: when we're the ones buying something, we care about price, too. So here's our first suggestion for handling a buyer's focus on price: get over it!

Now that that's out of the way, we can give you more practical advice, which is summed up in the chapter title: sell value, not price. Unless you can present price in the context of your overall value, you'll get stuck in an adversarial trap where the buyer sees your products and services as commodities. Luckily, you're not stuck there. By the end of this chapter, you will know how to sufficiently convey value and price as part of the big picture, not in isolation.

We knew this book would be incomplete without addressing the issue of price and value as perceived by the buyer. Our informal research confirmed this: when we invited sales leaders to share any challenges they faced with buyers, the response we received more than any other was pricing pressure.

What might surprise you, though, is the primary source of this pressure. In the book *Inside the Buyer's Brain* (Hinge, 2013), Hinge Marketing's research shows that more than 50 percent of sellers say that pricing is a key driver in the buyer's decision. However, only 28 percent of buyers say price is a key driver in the decision process. Given these findings, then, we might conclude that price matters most when the *seller* believes that price matters most.

When your clients or prospects do start to give you a hard time about price, it is often a sign that you did a less-than-stellar job of helping them see your value. You might see pricing pressure for the initial sale, or you might see it when clients are ready to reorder. We'll cover both situations in this chapter.

See the Big Picture

Ian had an opportunity to speak with Bob, the founder and CEO of a regional architecture and design firm. Bob's firm specializes in designing the interior of commercial office buildings. Bob was complaining that his clients just care about price. Ian asked Bob, "How much does your typical project generate in fees?" Bob explained that his company would like to earn about $4.50 per square foot for a typical project, but they can't charge more than $3.50 per square foot. Their typical project is a scope of 20,000 square feet. So, his clients and their representatives have trouble paying Bob's firm $90,000 versus the $70,000 they believe they should be paying.

In this situation, the buyer is shocked by the $20,000 difference and wonders if the seller is nuts:

Buyer's Perspective: *Wow! Bob is $20,000 more than my alternatives. He must be insane. Doesn't he want our business? Salespeople seem to be offended when we need to go with the lowest cost. I understand that everyone likes to be a premium product, but don't they have cost constraints when they buy at their companies? I have a board to answer to, and they are ALWAYS concerned about cost.*

The seller is thinking, "Are you kidding me? You are embarking on a multimillion-dollar investment, and you are giving us grief over $20,000? Why are they squeezing us? Don't they realize that we'll deliver a much better result for their project?"

Discount vs. Bob in Isolation

Architecture and Design

■ Discount Architects   ■ Bob the Architect

What's going on here, and how can this gap be bridged?

The problem is that Bob generally presents his fee independently of the overall project costs and the long-term cost of the broader solution. Clients are about to make a multimillion-dollar investment, but that aspect hasn't been mentioned.

Share the Big Picture

In order to work on the same side, the buyer and seller need to view the purchasing decision through a common lens—something that's clearly not happening yet. To get there, both buyer and seller need to think about this project in terms of the big picture.

Bob said that his company's typical project is about 20,000 square feet. Here is the information Bob shared about his business.

How long is the typical lease for a 20,000-square-foot building?	10 years
What is the average cost of the lease per square foot in this market?	$40
On average, how much does construction cost per square foot?	$50 to $85

Doing simple math, we see that the end-customer's lease cost would be $800,000 per year. The 10-year lease would be worth $8 million—plus annual increases. Construction (using the low end of the range at $50) would be $1 million. So the total transaction at this point would be $9 million. Brokerage fees and annual increases would easily bring the total cost to more than $10 million.

If Bob priced his work at $4.50 per square foot, the fee would be $90,000—less than 1 percent of the overall transaction value. The difference is so small that it's barely visible in the following chart.

Discount vs. Bob in Context

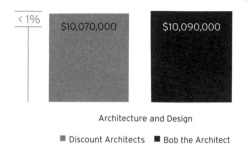

Architecture and Design

■ Discount Architects   ■ Bob the Architect

Changing the context of the architecture fee changes our perspective, doesn't it? Let's get back to Bob and see how this change works.

Ian asked Bob, "What is the single greatest factor in whether or not the space is successful for the client?" Bob said, "The architecture and design." Ian asked, "Do you really think that the client would make a decision that could put the project at risk to save $20,000 on a $10 million project?" Bob said, "If the client saw it in the big picture of the larger project, then of course they would pay a bit more."

Here is the key: *It is not the client's job to see the big picture.* It is Bob's job to ensure that the client sees Bob's price in the context of the overall project and its value.

Compared to $70,000, Bob's fee of $90,000 sounds high. Compared to $10,000,000, the difference appears insignificant.

In this example, Bob can illustrate the cost of his services in relation to the overall scope of the project. Doing so allows the buyer to see that the relative difference in fees is almost irrelevant. Just about anyone would be willing to spend an additional $20,000, on top of $10 million, if they felt they would get a better result from that investment.

Framing Total Cost and Total Value

The old-school salesperson had a goal of selling at all costs. Same Side Selling is ensuring that your clients or prospects see that you are looking out for their best interests. The total cost of ownership is their "real" cost. The initial purchase price might cover your transaction, but not their eventual investment. It is your job to illustrate all of the costs of their project—even the ones that you don't control. The self-interested salesperson might be afraid to open the client's eyes to other costs, but the Same Side Selling professional recognizes that transparency is the key to value and to long-term business relationships.

When Ian was looking to purchase a luxury sports sedan, he met with David Waghelstein, president of MemberCar (MemberCar.com). Let's face it: most people do not have a positive impression of car salespeople. One of David's differentiators is that he has a reputation for being honest, which might not be so interesting if he was in a different industry. We're not suggesting that he'll tell you your baby is ugly, but he will not sneak something by you just to get a sale.

The car Ian was considering was a few years old and had only twelve thousand miles on it. When Ian drove it home on a test drive, his twelve-year-old son was jumping up and down in the front yard with excitement. Ian was ready to make the purchase, but when he returned to MemberCar, David said, "Ian, just know that this type of vehicle is likely to have annual maintenance costs of more than the car payments. It's not meant to be driven as your primary car. I just don't want you to buy the car and regret that decision later." The maintenance costs had not entered Ian's mind.

Ian ultimately decided not to buy that car from David, but Ian has referred dozens of customers to MemberCar. David and

MemberCar earned a customer and referral source for life. By ensuring that Ian saw all of the potential costs, David avoided a potential disaster and earned Ian's trust for a lifetime. In Same Side Selling, you need to seek those things that could create a less-than-outstanding experience for your client. It is your job to ensure that the buyer does not feel burned by something, whether that something is in or out of your direct control. Presenting those potential challenges to your client elevates your value and demonstrates that you put their interests above your own.

Address the Total Cost and Assess the Buyer's Needs

Getting the total cost on the table sounds easy, right? All you need to do is create a spreadsheet that shows every cost related to your work. You can then hand it to the client, and she will understand everything, right? WRONG. Getting the total cost on the table is a collaborative process. It's most important that the buyer understand and take ownership of the total costs. However, the seller can add value by guiding the collaborative process to identify total costs.

Here is where you can use third-party stories again. One such story might sound like:

> "For a recent client, in addition to our software license of $200,000, they also needed a server for $20,000, and they needed some additional training and development totaling about $100,000. How similar might those costs be for you?"

Know where your solutions add the most value, and where you are just like the rest of the competitors in the field. If the client takes advantage of your enhanced capabilities, then you are worth every penny of premium. But if they want only the basics, recognize that the client might not be able to justify the additional investment. The important thing here is to uncover the truth. This is another place where you can use a third-party story:

> "Some of our clients just want the bare basics. In other cases, they tell us that the impact we can have by addressing Situation X is potentially more valuable than the rest of the project. How does that align with your situation?"

If the client doesn't see value in your differentiators, there are three potential outcomes:

- The person with whom you are speaking is not personally affected, and you might need to expand your contacts to find people within the organization who will care about those enhanced capabilities;
- The client does not need your differentiators, and he might struggle to pay a premium for something he doesn't see as valuable; or
- The client does not value your unique attributes, and you have to decide if you still want the business competing as a commodity against others. This decision gets back to knowing your value and working within opportunities most likely to value your strengths.

When you simply tell the buyer about the big picture and the related costs, you might get his verbal agreement but not his heart. What we mean is that he may give you superficial agreement but not really believe it. When it comes time to defend the investment, the buyer might not have the confidence needed to go to bat for the solution.

Make it clear when someone would pay a premium and when the cheap alternative might be good enough. "If you are simply using our services for this, then you might be better served with a low-cost provider like X or Y—I can see that. Our clients are really looking for this added benefit, and that's when we provide the lowest overall cost."

Whatever you do, avoid the temptation to fake the analysis. Jack was helping a client with a purchase, and the seller provided a cost model that was supposed to look like it was created internally. When Jack and his client discovered that it was simply fabricated by the salesperson, it created mistrust, and they went with another vendor. Once you violate a prospect's trust, there is not much you can do to recover.

Pitfalls of Getting the Total Cost out in the Open

You know your products and services, and you might believe that your clients will receive great benefits. However, there are two common pitfalls associated with presenting costs, impact, and value. Both pitfalls involve making assumptions about the buyer.

Phantom Savings

Let's say Bill has software that allows each employee to perform a certain task in 3 minutes, when it would normally take 13 minutes. Let's say that this task is performed once a day. Software sellers often use this model to justify investments. "I can save you ten minutes a day for each employee. If you have fifty employees, that's more than eight hours a day. If your average labor costs you $1,000 per week, then this software will save you the cost of one employee annually."

There's one problem. What's the chance that the company will eliminate the position from the company? Though the software might save the company a day's worth of labor, it is unlikely to result in the company's eliminating one position from their payroll. Phantom savings like those are not sufficient. Get back to issue, impact, and importance. Remember Finding Impact Together.

> **Buyer's Perspective:** *You are telling me that you will save us ten minutes per day. We're not going to eliminate a position because each person saved ten minutes. My bet is that my employees will just have another ten minutes of time on their hands to surf the Internet. I'm not willing to invest money for that.*

Not Everyone Has the Same Impact from the Same Issue

Ian traveled to China to help an organization that was selling a solution for reducing medication errors. The vendor employed an expert who researched the impact of medication errors. He was considered one of the top experts on medication errors in North America. The expert explained to the people running the Chinese hospital how much each medication error costs. He also explained the percentage of errors that even the best hospitals make every day. The expert stated that if a hospital saw one million patients, it would incur over $4 million in medication error costs. This figure, of course, made the investment of $500,000 trivial.

There was one problem. The only person who believed the calculation was the one presenting it. Ultimately, the client did not believe the numbers (nor were they accurate in China), and the hospital declined to implement the technology. Though the presenter was an expert in North America, the story did not apply to China. Similarly, recognize that although your solution might be of great value to Company X, it might not have the same impact on Company Y.

On the opposite extreme, consider the pharmaceutical industry. Large pharmaceutical companies estimate that for an important drug, each day on the market equates to at least $1 million in revenue. Some salespeople question whether the $1 million-a -day number is real. But the pharmaceutical companies believe it because once their drug patent expires (this take 17 years), then generic companies can produce the drug, and the margins for the drug decline dramatically. Pharmaceutical companies will spend large sums of money if they are convinced that you can shorten the time to market for new drugs.

The key is to sell in a way that supports your clients' beliefs, not what you think their beliefs should be.

Cost Too High? Expand the Scope

The natural inclination of most sellers when faced with pricing pressure is either to discount the price or to reduce the scope of the opportunity. Though it might seem counterintuitive, one of your best options might be to expand the scope to create more value. To see how this strategy can work, consider the following example.

Excella Consulting was working with a client who said their price was too high. What Excella co-founder Jeff Gallimore did next might surprise you. He acknowledged that given the scope of the project, the client might not get sufficient value from Excella to justify the additional expense. (Companies that need project management professionals but don't want to hire them directly can "rent" them from Excella Consulting.) Through discussions with the client, Jeff saw another project for which Excella could deliver value.

Jeff explained to the client that they could expand the scope to include that other project at a marginal increase in investment. Excella could use the same project management approach to oversee both projects, and the client would still get top-tier service and value with a marginal increase in cost. While every other vendor was competing on the narrow scope, Excella worked on the same side as the client to meet more of the client's needs.

Not only did Excella earn the project, but the client valued the fact that Excella had the vision to see where else they could help the client. The expanded scope allowed the client to justify the increased investment and appreciate how Excella created more value per invested dollar than the lower-priced alternatives would have.

Compare on Value, Not Price

Sometimes your cost is the same as the competing alternatives. In that situation, you can either try to compete on price or compete on value. The problem with competing on price is that the customer who switches from another vendor to you because of price will also switch from you in the future for the same reason.

Consider the example of Calmac, a manufacturer of energy storage solutions. Calmac's innovative technology helps clients heat and cool their commercial buildings far more efficiently than traditional cooling and heating systems. Owners of a typical building could save 20 percent or more on their annual energy costs with a Calmac solution, which often does not cost more to buy or install than other systems. Even clients that replace their existing systems break even on the investment in less than three years. Not bad, eh?

The Bigger Big Picture

As compelling as the cost and energy savings are, there is more to the Calmac story. Energy savings are just the tip of the iceberg (pun intended). When landlords implement energy storage, it helps the building attain energy efficiency certification. Calmac's energy storage systems deliver cooler air than traditional systems do, so buildings are more comfortable for their tenants.

Efficiency improvements and cooler air are benefits in addition to the reduced costs. The decision to use energy storage from companies like Calmac can lead to higher occupancy, better tenant retention, and higher demand, all of which drives higher rents. When a solution offers not simply lower costs but also higher revenue, it becomes even more compelling for the buyer.

Never get caught in a discussion of price when you have the opportunity to discuss value. Be clear about where you add value for your client, and engage in meaningful discussions to ensure that you share a common belief about the reality of that value. Remember, if the client doesn't seem to have the vision, this might be a good time to share a third-party story about how similar organizations have realized value.

Address Objections in Advance to Avoid the Eleventh-Hour Disaster

There are common, recurring obstacles that come up with almost every large deal (some of these come up regardless of deal size). Following are three common scenarios and suggestions on how to overcome them.

Before the Deal Is Done: Enter Procurement

You've done a great job building value with the person who's responsible for a specific line of business in a client organization. This buyer might be the head of human resources, compliance, sales, or another department. As the deal nears the conclusion, the buyer introduces Jack from procurement. Jack expects that any reasonable vendor will give them a 10 percent discount on the price you have already agreed to. (Ian is taking cheap shots at Jack here!) By anticipating this possibility, sellers can be prepared to defend their price:

> "Sometimes in an organization your size, Purchasing will get involved in the end, not realizing that you and I have already worked hard to get you the best pricing possible. They'll ask for a 10 percent discount, and when they don't get it, they might think that we are inflexible or that you haven't done your due diligence. We've even seen that result in companies choosing a vendor that would deliver less impact. Is that at all a concern here, and are there steps we can take to ensure that your purchasing team will feel confident about the value and the process?"

Before the Deal Is Done: Enter Legal

Everyone is in agreement, and Legal simply needs to review the final details. It turns out, though, that Legal or Accounting demands a change in some of the terms of the deal. The change requires you to incur additional expenses and alters the fundamental business model. What was going to be a fair deal is now structured so you fear that you'll lose money if even the slightest snag comes up—which is sure to happen.

Here is one way to address those potential disruptions before they occur:

> "Sometimes in an organization your size, Legal or Accounting will have some last-minute changes that might hamper our ability to work effectively with you. Sometimes those discussions can turn our joint collaboration into an adversarial trap. What's the chance of that happening in your organization? If it does come up, how should we tackle it together?"

After the Deal Is Done, They Suddenly Want a Discount

For the initial purchase, you help the buyer realize that what he thought his company needed would not have addressed their needs. You engineer a wonderful solution, and the client rewards you by not focusing on the lowest cost and by appreciating the value you brought in solving his company's problems. Six months later, it is time for the company to reorder. You get a phone call from Purchasing (not the people for whom you delivered magic the first time), and they want to order more of the same thing they bought six months ago. They have researched alternative vendors, and now they want you to sell to them for 20 percent less than the original price. It seems that another vendor, who had not invested the time to devise the solution, is willing to deliver that solution for 20 percent less than you are.

> **Buyer's Perspective:** *When our board of directors or CFO mandates spending cuts, we look at our vendor expenses. After the fat is cut, we sometimes have to talk to valued vendors about reducing their pricing or figuring out some sort of arrangement so we can keep working with them. I know they hate that; we hate it, too. But when we keep getting sales calls from competing vendors that appear to offer better pricing, we need some way to justify the rates internally.*

You won't always be able to ensure loyalty or appreciation for past service. But you can often reframe how a buyer sees the cost by pointing to value in the future:

> "After the initial purchase, sometimes reorders will get pushed to Purchasing. Reordering the same item again might not always be the right solution. Just as in this case, where what you initially requested was not the right fit, we want to ensure that we don't simply ship more of the same only to discover later that you would have been better served by something else. If Purchasing contacts us independently from you, how should we get you involved to ensure that you get the right solution?"

Notice that in each case, you are putting yourself and the buyer on the same side of the table to solve the negotiating puzzle. As you do this (and resist the temptation to take on a negotiation death match), the buyer will often guide you through the minefield so both of you can come out on the other end unscathed.

Put Same Side Selling to Work

Value is not a simple presentation of price. Rather, it is a collaborative discussion with your clients to identify, present, and confirm the value of their projects. This conversation often involves a reframing to see the "big picture" of total costs and total value. When you take a Same Side approach, you understand the client's challenge and impact and can use that understanding to make sure the conversation does not simply focus on the purchase price.

- ✔ Always present price in the context of the big picture to include the client's resources and other costs that are required for the client to buy and implement what you are selling.
- ✔ When confronted with price objections, be sure that you and the buyer are working together to evaluate the total cost, not just the initial purchase cost.
- ✔ Know your own strengths, and focus on the opportunities where you can deliver the greatest value to clients.
- ✔ Avoid the adversarial trap of arguing value against your client. Get on the same side, and don't be afraid to walk away if you cannot deliver value.
- ✔ Define the most common last-minute objections and obstacles, and address them with your customer.

CHAPTER 9
Deliver Impact

If you navigated through your sales process with Same Side Selling and found a fit with the buyer, then congratulations are in order! The sale is made, the deal is done, and the ink is dry. The moment is worth savoring.

Remember, though: the sale is not the finish line.

The sale itself is not the goal. The sale is a necessary step *toward* the goal. Early in the sales process, you worked collaboratively with the buyer to Find Impact Together (FIT), and you defined the value of your solution. Now the goal is to deliver value and ensure that your client realizes the outcome or results you discussed. Whether your title includes "Sales," "Operations," or anything else, the point of selling is to deliver impact.

Delivery is the great payoff for your work in building the puzzle. After so much effort to Find Impact Together, you now get to realize the benefit of the impact. For a seller, delivering impact opens the gateway to repeat and referral business. But failing to deliver opens the gateway to Hell! OK, that's overly dramatic, but while we're on the subject:

> A young man has a rare opportunity to visit Hell before he dies. In a tour guided by the Devil himself, the man sees people playing golf, eating gourmet dinners, and generally having a wonderful time. "This isn't so bad," he thinks to himself.
>
> Many years later (after a sinful, selfish life), the man dies and returns to Hell, but this time the scene is quite different. People are sick, tortured, and miserable. The man tracks down the Devil and says, "Where are the golf courses? Where are the gourmet meals?" The Devil admits, "Oh, that was just our sales process. Now you're in customer service."

This old-time joke makes people laugh because the example hits home. Too often, companies fail to deliver what they promised. The fact that the term *Caveat Emptor*—Buyer Beware—has been used since the 1400s reflects the long, deep history of the adversarial trap.

To avoid under-delivering, we look at how to continue Same Side Selling after the sale itself, through the kickoff and implementation. We discuss how to handle conflicts and other problems that intrude during delivery. We also look at enjoying the benefit by celebrating the project's success and encouraging referrals and repeat business.

Stay Involved

After a sale, there is often some sort of handoff from the salesperson to an account manager or project manager who takes responsibility for the customer relationship. This transition is delicate. It can lead directly to the adversarial trap if the buyer thinks the person with whom he has built a relationship was there only to win the sale.

> **Buyer's Perspective:** *After we spent nearly two months making a buying decision, it blew my mind that Ed, the salesperson, didn't come to our implementation meetings. His absence was hard for me to get over, and it didn't help that we had to explain to someone else several things that Ed and I had spent hours discussing. I kept thinking, "If Ed were here, we wouldn't have to review this again."*

The person who led the sales process should always be engaged throughout the project. If this isn't your company's policy, do it anyway.

An ongoing presence and communication will be natural in Same Side Selling. After investing effort and time to pursue a potential fit, and then finding that the offering does in fact provide value, most sellers will want to see that value become reality.

Staying in touch with the buyer does not have to mean a huge investment of time. Even when the salesperson has no formal role after the sale, it is simple to reach out and check in with the buyer. Here are a couple examples of how the salesperson can start a check-in conversation with the client:

> "Bill, it's been two months since we implemented. I've heard good things, but I wanted to hear it from you. On a scale of 1 to 10, how would you rate how things have gone?"

> "Louise, I know our operations team is taking good care of you, but I really enjoyed learning about your company and I miss our conversations. I would love to hear about whether our solution is turning out as well as we thought it would."

Buyer's Perspective: *When we were just a prospect, the salesperson was calling me three times a day. Now that we've said yes, I can't even get a return phone call. I understand that their primary job is to get new clients, but it would be great if they gave as much attention to current clients as they do to potential clients.*

It's also very worthwhile to stay in touch long after the client project has concluded. Ian makes it a policy to check in with all of his old clients at least twice a year. There is no agenda for these calls other than to maintain a relationship and see how things are going, but it's surprising how many of them lead to more business. The important part is to ask about the clients' results and the challenges they are facing, not to ask leading questions that sound like "Got any money lying around for us?"

Bringing Others to the Same Side

Implementation often means bringing new people onto the project, particularly if some stakeholders were not involved in the buying process. The result is that even after the sale, some of the key people on the buyer's team might not yet be working from the same side. They might have an adversarial mindset toward you and your team, or have a habitual mistrust of vendors. They might even have preferred another vendor that was not selected. Whatever is going on, you need to work to get everyone up to speed and on the same side.

This continuation of the sales process is essential to delivering impact. Building consensus after the sale can be more challenging than reaching agreement on the purchase of your product or service. Each individual in the buyer's organization faces competing priorities and demands. Yet for many of you—especially those in professional services—your project is destined to fail if you do not get the people in the buyer's organization on the same side with you. So let's discuss ways to get them there.

Seek Risks and Plan for Them

As you bring other people into the project, it is not a time for rosy optimism and the projection that everything will go perfectly. A far better way to disarm them and build teamwork is to be realistic about the effort required and the risks you might encounter.

186

There is a path to success for every project. Similarly, there are impediments that could derail just about any well-designed plan. Seek out the risks that could bring everything to a grinding halt. Develop a list of the specific steps that could spell trouble. Work together with the buyer to determine the best way to avoid those problems. In Chapter 8, we explained how to address potential objections to avoid last-minute disasters; you'll use a similar process now to mention potential snags and decide in advance how to resolve them.

The first company Ian started earned a contract with a large insurance company. As part of the project kickoff meeting, Ian asked the room of more than twenty people, "How many of you have ever been involved in a perfect project?" The attendees chuckled. Of course, nobody raised their hand. Ian continued, "Me neither. So, before we get started, I'd like to lay out the process for how we'll work together when one of us feels that something is wrong with the project or system." Ian spelled out the process (including calling Ian at step 3) to resolve a potential problem. Ian gave each team member a laminated card that outlined the steps for resolving glitches in the project.

The pilot was launched, and about ten days later the system stopped working. The client, Jim, called Ian and, with a tone of concern and angst in his voice, said, "The system crashed. We're freaking out. I'm at step 3, and I'm calling you." Ian explained that as outlined in the document, he would get back to the client within two hours. As you might imagine, Ian's company's internal time requirement was much shorter (within one hour). About forty minutes later, after discovering that Jim's own database engineers had caused the problem when they changed the structure of the database, Ian called and said, "We've uncovered the problem, and the system should be restored within an hour." Jim said, "While waiting for your call, my team said it was our fault. Is that true?" Ian responded by saying, "Our goal is to deliver a working solution. There will be times when your team fixes our errors or vice versa. All that matters is that we work together to get it working. We don't lose sleep over who made the mistake." Years later, when giving a stellar referral for Ian, Jim said to the potential client, "Not only do they do great work, but even when our own people messed up, they took responsibility."

Because everyone knew the plan for handling problems, Ian's client did not fly off the handle. Though he was concerned, he simply followed the plan and everyone was on the same page (or same side).

Practical Examples to Help the Buyer Avoid Pain

Suppose you sell technology solutions, and from experience you know that if the customer's staff does not attend training, the project is likely to fail. You might emphasize this to the buyer by saying, "We are going to design a great training program and have fantastic support. However, if people do not attend the training, it could make the rollout problematic. What can we do together to avoid that situation?"

If you run an accounting firm, you know that clients with incomplete information end up paying more in fees than those who are well organized. You might say, "Our clients who get us complete information by the seventh day of the month spend about 40 percent less than the ones who send us information a piece at a time throughout the month and with numerous changes."

When Jack led operations at an accounts-payable outsourcing company, one of the recurring sticky points of implementation was obtaining the interface file for the clients' ERP (enterprise resource planning) systems. The buyers of the solution were typically finance executives with no direct reports in the information technology department—the group responsible for creating the interface. After experiencing delays with several clients due to this specific problem, Jack and his team started raising this issue at the kickoff meeting as a key to success that often needed executive oversight. After Jack gave visibility and priority to that one step, the interface file rarely became a problem again.

For whichever problems you anticipate, you want the client to be an integral part of finding the solution. To get the client involved, try asking questions like these:

> "Given this schedule and these tasks, what risks do you see on your side?"

> "We'll be dependent on these specific individuals and groups at your company. Is there any reason to think that they might not be able to play their role well, and in the timeframe we have laid out?"

The process of identifying risks and addressing potential problems in advance is often that last "extra mile" that can make it much easier for your team to implement and deliver value. If you focus on your strengths, consistently qualify prospects, strive to find impact together, focus on value, and demonstrate restraint, you will grow revenue, lower operational costs, and stop wasting time chasing rainbows.

You will build a reputation for delivering value. Know that there will almost always be snags that get in the way of immediate success. Do not wait for the snags to happen. Instead, address the most common issues ahead of time.

The First Hundred Days

At the beginning of a project, you have an opportunity that you will never have again: the opportunity to make a first impression. Whether it's fair or not, many people at the buyer's organization will form their lasting opinion of you from the first few interactions.

Our friend Joey Coleman delivers a workshop called "The First 100 Days." Joey explains that the reason banks tend to give gifts and incentives to customers after one hundred days is that most business relationships that fail will fail in the first hundred days. If you make it past that point, you are likely to have earned a client for many years. Think about what you could do in the first hundred days to make the buyer's experience extraordinary. We're not suggesting that you give everyone a new toaster, as banks used to do. Just remember that simple steps often produce a lasting impact.

For example, Ian's wife, Deborah, took her car to an auto repair shop for routine service. Three days later, the service manager took the simple step of calling Deborah to ensure that she was 100 percent satisfied with their work. Deborah mentioned that the tire pressure was low, but she didn't know if checking that was part of their service. The manager said, "It certainly should be. When are you going to be near our shop? Just call me from the car and we'll take care of it without your needing to even get out of the vehicle."

Prior to their call, Deborah had thought, "I just had my car serviced and they didn't check the tire pressure." After the call, she said, "I love how they follow up." Deborah went from being a negative to a positive reference as the result of a 60-second phone call.

Responding to the Adversarial Trap

A great start can set the tone for a solid long-term relationship, but it is no guarantee that things won't change. Over the course of a customer relationship, the adversarial trap threatens in various ways. When it does, you'll need to watch your step because the wrong move could make things much worse. Each time a shadow of the us-versus-them mentality creeps in, you can choose to respond in a way that either pushes the situation farther on the path to an adversarial minefield or gets everyone back on the same side. Here are a few examples:

Someone Tries to Sabotage the Project

Situation: Shortly after the project begins, a department manager named Chris, inside your client's organization, begins holding back information you need in order to succeed.

Adversarial response [to one or more of Chris's coworkers]: "Chris has not provided us with this information, and without it, we are stuck."

Same Side response [to Chris]: "Chris, I'm guessing that we have done something that has caused you to mistrust us. Rest assured that our goal, just like yours, is the success of this project. What can we do to make you and your team comfortable working with us?"

Explanation: In the adversarial response, you throw Chris under the bus. You assign blame, accurately in this case, to Chris. The problem is that your response draws attention to the adversarial trap and is likely to escalate the situation. Chris will likely never be on your side. In the Same Side response, you take responsibility, assuming that you or your team did something that caused his reluctance. You then ask Chris for the explanation and solution.

A Minor Snag Gets Blown out of Proportion

Situation: Six months into the project, someone discovers an error. Quickly, the internal department that wanted to do the project without your help has suggested that your work is substandard and that nothing you do can be trusted.

Adversarial response: "This issue is not a big deal. We did everything else correctly, and the other group is just trying to latch onto a trivial issue to derail the project."

Same Side response: "After so many accomplishments on this project, we are embarrassed to have made a mistake like this. No matter how insignificant some people might think it is, each mistake is an indication that we might need to make adjustments in order to meet your goals. We have drafted a plan to ensure that this does not happen again. We want to get your input to ensure that we have not overlooked anything important. But I have to ask: The fact that we had this one mistake, does that mean we cannot earn your trust going forward?"

Explanation: In the adversarial response, you defend your position and sound threatened. In the Same Side response, you own up to the mistakes, engage the client team so they accept your solution, ask if this misstep prevents them from earning your trust going forward, and give them a chance to resolve their concerns. Remember, your goal is to simply get to the truth. Better to know now, rather than later, if the relationship is beyond repair.

If the relationship began from the same side as you applied the principles and tactics explained in the previous chapters, these occasions at the brink of the adversarial trap will be rare. You will have established the practice of Finding Impact Together. The maintenance work is easier than the initial work, but it still requires care.

The Client Wants to Expand the Scope Without Raising the Price

Too often, when faced with confrontation from buyers, sellers can inadvertently focus on their own situation instead of on the customer. This is especially common when it sounds like the client is asking you to do more for the same money: "We assume that this other component is also included. We're going to need that." Worried about a change in scope, you might respond with statements like:

> "We agreed to do X in the contract. Now you are asking us to do something different."

If you find yourself being pulled into an adversarial stance, remember to focus on the client's outcome instead of on your own issues. A Same Side response to the buyer's request for new products or services might be:

> "I know that originally we determined that your goal was to accomplish Z. I want to be sure we are all pursuing the same goal. Can we take a moment to define what we hope to accomplish and how we will measure success in this specific area?"

In this example, you focus on the outcome and the client's needs first. The idea here is to get both parties on the same page to understand a) the original scope, b) the change in scope, and c) the impact and goals associated with the new scope, so that together you and the client can determine the value of that change. If it is important enough, then both parties can agree to a plan moving forward. Sometimes after a brief discussion, together you realize that someone fabricated a need that is not really important, and the client decides that he doesn't need the additional component after all. If it turns out that he does need it, though, the discussion helps him better understand its value. Either way, you remain on the same side, rather than sliding into the adversarial trap.

Finishing Strong

We believe that practicing Same Side Selling will help you achieve more success with your clients than ever before. As you approach the conclusion of a project or client engagement and you see that you have delivered impact, this is a time for recognition, appreciation, and celebration. This is more than just feel-good-ism or a hollow trophy ceremony. It is strategic.

Celebration provides a time to tell a story with a beginning, middle, and end. The beginning was the problem that was causing the client pain, difficulty, or loss of some kind. That problem also led the client to you, and you mutually discovered a good fit. The middle was your working together. The ending is the outcome, where the problem is solved.

All this reminds the client that he made a good decision to hire you. It is a decision that he could make again if the fit was right. It is a decision that he could easily recommend to another company.

The celebration is a perfect time to remind the client that he is more than a paycheck to you. You might find yourself making statements like these:

> "Since you were our first client in this segment, this was a great opportunity for us."

> "We learned so much about XX in this project; I know we will use that soon."

> "It's been a great business partnership, and a great friendship."

That last sentence about friendship might have seemed forced or strange when you first cracked the cover of *Same Side Selling*. Our sincere hope is that it now seems quite natural. Once you start selling from the same side, it's easier to develop friendly relationships with your prospects and customers.

As we know, the best projects solve specific problems with specific solutions. There's a big difference between a client saying, "They helped us increase our sales" and saying, "They helped us increase revenue by 18 percent in six months." Not every circumstance is as easy to quantify as revenue, but the goal is to define results as specifically as possible. Doing so benefits not just your client but you, too, because you then—with the client's permission—have material for a case study.

The Same Side Case Study

Case studies can become a valuable tool for sharing third-party stories with others. However, the typical case study follows a format that does not help the sales process:

20% Client background
60% Description of solution and what you did for the client
10% Benefits of the solution
10% About your company

The problem with the traditional approach is that it is focused on what you did, more than it is on why the client needed it. A reader of the traditional case study would know little about the problem and everything about your solution. But that formula is not aligned with the way buyers make decisions. Instead, consider the following Same Side Selling case study format:

10% Client background
50% Client issue, impact, and importance
40% Outcome of solution

195

This format aligns with the way buyers make decisions. You share the impact and importance so that a reader facing the same issue might realize the impact that it could have. Someone reading the case study who has a similar issue will be intrigued by the topic, discover the problem's potential impact, and have a sense of how life could get better with your help.

Note, though, that the solution for the client in the case study might not be the right solution for other clients. Including the solution, instead of the outcome of the solution, might create confusion. If readers face similar challenges, and they want to learn about the solution, they'll contact you. That is a good thing, right?

Within the outcome section, we recommend that you include ONE SENTENCE acknowledging your work.

Seek Referrals to Share the Results

Typical sellers ask for referrals in a way that rarely provides positive results. For example, sellers might ask, "Can you think of other people we should talk to about our product or service?" This type of question from the seller can immediately trigger an adversarial trap.

> **Buyer's Perspective**: *When you ask me if I can refer you to others, what I hear is, "Can you give me the names, numbers, and email addresses of people I can contact twice a day for rest of their lives until they buy or go into hiding?" I'm not signing up for that.*

Same Side Selling allows you to ask for referrals in a way that helps people feel comfortable, while setting the proper tone for an introduction. Once you have successfully delivered the promised outcome and resolved the issue that was causing impact, you are ready to proceed. The way you approach the client might sound like this:

> "When we started this project, I know you were facing Issue X that was having Impact Y on the organization. On a scale of 0 to 10, how well did we address that challenge?"

You should already know what the answer will be, and probably do not want to ask for referrals if the client's answer would be below an 8. Assuming that you get a favorable response to the question, then ask,

> "Can you think of one or two other people inside or outside of your organization who might be facing a similar challenge? I don't know if we can produce the same outcome for them, but I'd be happy to speak with them to see if we can help."

You can offer to draft a referral email for the client that says,

> "I want to introduce you to Pat. We were facing Issue X, and Pat's company helped us overcome that challenge quickly and effectively. I recall that you may have been facing a similar issue. Pat said they can't help everyone facing that issue, but they would be happy to speak with you to see if they can help."

Notice that the focus is on helping to address an issue. The note did not say, "We bought XYZ from Pat. Get your checkbook. Maybe you can buy it, too."

When your client agrees to the introduction, get a bit more specific:

> "Is that an introduction you feel comfortable making within the next two weeks? Would you prefer to make the introduction in person, over the phone, or via email?"

Once you get the introduction, you are at step 1 of Same Side Selling. The beauty of focusing on results is that you create a model of Find Impact—Deliver Results—Earn Referrals—Repeat.

Put Same Side Selling to Work

It would be a shame to follow Same Side Selling to the end and not deliver results for the client. By staying involved, seeking risks that could jeopardize a successful outcome, and ensuring that you deliver a great experience in the first hundred days, you will earn the opportunity for repeat and referral business. You can also capture your client's success in a *Same Side Selling* case study that will help other prospects realize how important it is to solve a problem similar to the one you solved for a client.

- ✔ Set an organizational requirement to have the salesperson present at the kick-off meeting.
- ✔ Once a project begins, be sure to call the client and confirm progress, or uncover anything that may not be going according to plan.
- ✔ Make a list of the challenges that can get in the way of success, and plan how to handle them with the buyer.
- ✔ Define six things you will do in the first hundred days to create a remarkable experience.
- ✔ Once your project is complete, work with your client to document the tangible results.
- ✔ Consider submitting your client's company for an award in their industry (especially if your solution may have played a part in increasing their eligibility for the award).
- ✔ Draft a case study, following the Same Side Selling case study format and focusing primarily on the client's issue and impact. (Remember to get the client's permission to distribute the case study.)
- ✔ Contact a prior client who had a successful project and see if she can identify one or two other companies that might be facing a similar challenge.

CHAPTER 10
Recap and Learning Points

❖

Our goal in writing *Same Side Selling* was to provide a framework to improve the relationship between buyers and sellers so both parties can reach a better outcome. We hope you can see how Same Side Selling provides an integrity-based approach for buyers and sellers to avoid playing games and to work collaboratively to put puzzles together where there is a good fit.

When you take the time to appreciate your unique value, focus on the right opportunities, uncover the truth, and then share your wisdom, you will find yourself on the same side of the table as the buyer. The buyer will appreciate your solution's fit and will better understand your value. When you achieve results, the client will be happy to guide you to other people or companies who can benefit from your help.

Chapter Summaries

We included this chapter as a way to help you find the sections you want to review. Let's start with the big picture:

The goal of Same Side Selling is to efficiently build long-term client relationships that are highly profitable for the seller and highly valuable for the buyer.

The approach to the goal is to stay in a cooperative, collaborative posture with the client throughout the sales process and to avoid the adversarial trap.

Now on to the chapter summaries:

Chapter 1: Stop Playing Games

The problem: People approach buying and selling with an adversarial mindset.

Key insight: The *us-versus-them* mentality that's the hallmark of the adversarial trap weakens negotiation strength, leads to longer sales cycles, and adds pricing pressure.

Key takeaways:
- Solving a puzzle is a better—more collaborative—metaphor than playing a game.
- Use the reminders "solving, not selling" and "FIT: Finding Impact Together" to stay focused on the buyer's problems.

Chapter 2: Be Unique

The problem: Too many companies try to be all things to all buyers rather than embracing their unique qualities and abilities.

Key insight: The most successful sellers prize depth rather than breadth by limiting themselves to the clients and situations for which they can deliver the most impact.

Key takeaways:
- A narrow focus builds credibility and speeds the selling process, whereas offering too wide a scope of services can erode trust.
- To find out where your business can have the most impact, find out what your customers are sick and tired of. (What's their elevator rant?)
- Use the Same Side pitch format to describe whom you help, what you help them with, and why they need your help.
- Define where you want your prospects to allocate their hundred pennies of trust in an initial client meeting.

Chapter 3: Narrow Your Market

The problem: Sellers waste time and money investing in unsuitable prospects who might be interested in what the seller offers but might not be sufficiently motivated to invest in a solution.

Key insight: The most important question is not what a prospect needs but why she would buy. Pursuing prospects without understanding why they buy is extremely costly.

Key takeaways:

- To avoid chasing unsuitable opportunities and wasting time, embrace the second-best outcome of a quick disqualification of the prospect.
- Use the "Entice, Disarm, and Discover" process to shift a conversation from what buyers want to why they are interested in it.
- With your help, buyers can qualify themselves through self-evaluation and assignment selling.

Chapter 4: Get to the Truth

The problem: After finding a prospect that seems to have a problem they can solve, sellers often jump to a prescription of what to sell without a sufficient understanding of two essential buyer qualities: urgency and readiness.

Key insight: A thorough diagnosis is required to reduce risk, increase the chances of a successful outcome, and ensure that you deliver value.

Key takeaways:

- It's perilous to move forward with a faulty understanding of the buyer's needs.
- Use the issue/impact/importance framework to assess a prospect's urgency.

- Move forward with only those prospects who rate the importance of the issue as an 8, 9, or 10 on a 10-point scale. Rarely do prospects succeed in securing funding for projects where importance is rated at less than 8.
- Make sure you assess a prospect's readiness to implement your solution and capture value.

Chapter 5: Be an Educator

The problem: Sellers' reluctance to share expertise and information feeds the us-versus-them mentality and makes the sale less likely.

Key insight: By embracing the role of the teacher with your client and sharing information freely and effectively, you get on the same side.

Key takeaways:
- A strategy of trying to protect secrets will not work in today's world.
- You can use a third-party story to demonstrate expertise in a highly effective way.
- Your credentials and qualifications matter only in the context of the client's problem.
- Develop guidelines so you know where the line is between education and free consulting.

Chapter 6: Focus on the Fit

The problem: Buyers can get distracted or repelled by small details and lose sight of the true value the seller brings.

Key insight: The seller must keep buyers focused on the overall fit and value more than on features or attributes of the solution.

Key takeaways:
- Present your solution as results-based, not resource-based.
- Define the boundaries of expertise early in the relationship.
- When you're working with a buyer who is fixated on a specific technology or person, re-focus on the fit.

Chapter 7: Don't Force the Fit

The problem: Too often sellers force-fit their solution in an effort to make the sale; this hurts the buyer and the seller.

Key insight: It seems like a paradox, but one of the most powerful sales techniques is stepping back and admitting that the buyer may be better off with someone else's solution.

Key takeaways:
- Forcing the fit is a toxic shortcut that causes short-term and long-term problems.
- You can step back from the sale in a way that enhances authority and trust.
- By providing referrals, you can keep solving problems for buyers even when you don't sell to them.
- Refer correctly to avoid pitfalls and build your stature.

Chapter 8: Sell Value, Not Price

The problem: After a successful sales process, buyers apply pricing pressure that can threaten margins and kill deals.

Key insight: By framing value in the right way, sellers can avoid being commoditized or pushed out by the low-price bidder.

Key takeaways:

- Price matters most when the seller thinks price matters most. Your greatest differentiation will often come when clients see that you are looking out for their best interests.
- When your client is fixated on price, ensure that you have demonstrated your unique value as it applies to the client's situation.
- Embrace the difference between the lowest bid and the lowest long-term total cost. The initial purchase price is just one piece in the larger puzzle of cost.
- Provide buyers with the context they need to appreciate where you bring unique capabilities to solving their problem. Buyers may need to make the case for your products or services when you are not there.
- Define the most common objections, and address them on your terms, instead of waiting until clients bring them up. If you wait, you'll likely sound defensive no matter how deftly you handle the conversation.

Chapter 9: Deliver Results

The problem: Too many sellers think that the job is over when the sale is made.

Key insight: Success is measured not by sales, but by the impact the client achieves.

Key takeaways:

- The most critical "selling" may come after the deal is done as you implement your solution with the buyer's team.
- Prepare to navigate surprises that could threaten the success of the project.

- Keeping in touch with a client after the sale and engagement can present great opportunities for more impact and more sales.

A Message from Ian and Jack

Ian and Jack are in agreement with everything within *Same Side Selling*. We do not discuss persuasion, coercion, or deception. Everything we share is in the mutual interest of the buyer and seller. We believe that buyers and sellers alike can benefit from Same Side Selling—so much so that you should feel comfortable sharing the book with a buyer and explaining that this is the process you would like to follow. Buyers may decide to share this book with sellers and suggest, "This is how we would like to work with you."

Please share your successes and challenges so that we can continue to offer value. We would love to share your success stories with others, and we have set aside some space on SameSideSelling.com where we will publish stories of success for those who follow *Same Side Selling*. We especially like the stories in which there is feedback from both the seller and the buyer.

Wishing you happy solving and Same Side success!

—Ian and Jack